LUXURY HOUSES

TOSCANA

AT HOME WITH TUSCANY'S GREAT FAMILIES

photographed and edited by Etienne Hunyady
Texts by Kelley F. Hurst

teNeues

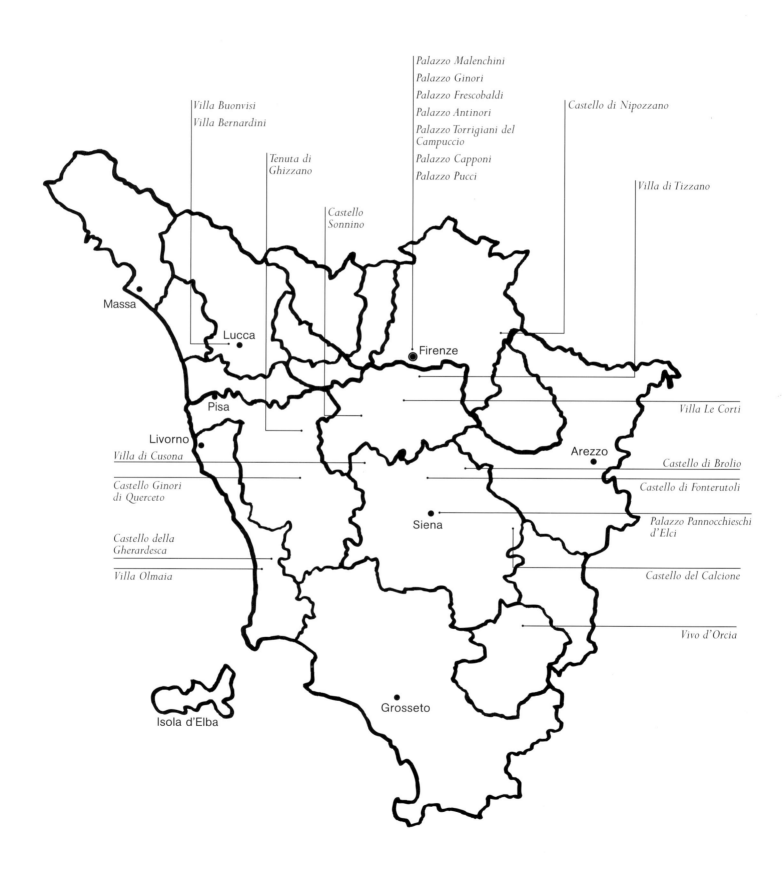

Palazzo Malenchini

Palazzo Ginori

Palazzo Frescobaldi

Palazzo Antinori

Palazzo Torrigiani del
Campuccio

Palazzo Capponi

Palazzo Pucci

Castello di Nipozzano

Villa Buonvisi

Villa Bernardini

Tenuta di
Ghizzano

Castello
Sonnino

Villa di Tizzano

Massa

Lucca

Firenze

Pisa

Villa Le Corti

Livorno

Arezzo

Villa di Cusona

Castello di Brolio

Castello Ginori
di Querceto

Castello di Fonterutoli

Siena

Palazzo Pannocchieschi
d'Elci

Castello della
Gherardesca

Castello del Calcione

Villa Olmaia

Vivo d'Orcia

Grosseto

Isola d'Elba

Luxury Houses

TOSCANA

Introduction	4
Malenchini	14
Palazzo Malenchini	
Ginori	24
Castello Ginori di Querceto	
Palazzo Ginori	
Pannocchieschi d'Elci	34
Palazzo Pannocchieschi d'Elci	
Frescobaldi	44
Palazzo Frescobaldi	
Castello di Nipozzano	
Mansi	54
Villa Buonvisi	
Villa Bernardini	
Ricasoli	64
Castello di Brolio	
Antinori	72
Palazzo Antinori	
Serristori	80
Villa Olmaia	
Torrigiani	90
Palazzo Torrigiani del Campuccio	
Corsini	100
Villa Le Corti	
Venerosi Pesciolini	114
Tenuta di Ghizzano	
Capponi	122
Palazzo Capponi	
Lotteringhi della Stufa	132
Castello del Calcione	
Guicciardini Strozzi	144
Villa di Cusona	
Pandolfini	156
Villa di Tizzano	
Cervini	170
Vivo d'Orcia	
Pucci	180
Palazzo Pucci	
de Renzis Sonnino	190
Castello Sonnino	
della Gherardesca	200
Castello della Gherardesca	
Mazzei	210
Castello di Fonterutoli	
Imprint	220

Toscan Luxury

Tuscan luxury is not a matter of ostentatious riches, or exhibitionism. First-time visitors to the large cities or small towns of Tuscany, starting out from Florence, are struck by the narrowness of the roads. The important palaces with their grand architecture and coats of arms are not readily visible; in fact, they are rarely seen unless one cares to actively look for them. The same is also true of many of the best-known series of frescoes, grandly painted on the cupolas and walls of palaces and cathedrals. Might this apparent shyness be blamed on technical ignorance? Might it be possible to accuse the artists and their clients of snobbery? No, it is a matter of substance. The rich and powerful of Tuscany, the Florentines and the Sienese, the nobles of Pisa and Volterra (especially these), required "essence" rather than "appearance." The choice of stone as the primary material for public and private buildings is a response to this specific need for substance, an intrinsic quality. Florence, Siena, and Arezzo are cities of stone, which also frames the most elegant marble façades.

The story of Tuscany's singular "luxury" may well be read in the story of the society in a centuries-old progression toward urban modernity. Starting from the original village—generally Roman, or in some cases Etruscan—towns originally inhabited by warriors and boasting rich strongholds of towers, one is surrounded by groups of functional houses for the *popolo minuto*, or craftsmen. The towers, with their vertical expansions and cumbersome military equipment, add little to the ostentation of riches, nor do the fortified castles of the countryside. But it was the countryside's own, "the new people," as Dante scornfully called them, who poured into Florence on the threshold of the 14th century, establishing commerce and trade, factories and banks. The families ennobled themselves rapidly with "coin in hand," which became the starting point for the economy and finance of an expanding Europe. In addition to paper money, the Florentines invented the *palazzo*, that repository of great cultural treasures. This new middle class produced craftsmen and artists of every type: sculptors, painters, bronze-workers, marble-workers, and carpenters. Between the 15th and 16th centuries, Arnolfo di Cambio and Brunelleschi, Michelangelo and Leonardo worked in Florence designing and building churches and palaces for the newly rich and old moneyed families, the pinnacle of a "made in Tuscany" prestige that dominated the international scene for at least three centuries. This is Florentine and Tuscan luxury.

The first palaces of the Renaissance revival in Florence belonged to the Medici, Rucellai, Pitti, Pazzi, Antinori, Strozzi, and Gondi. The splendor of their furnishings, the collections of sculpture and objects d'art, and the parks and gardens always culminated in the place of honor: the grand art gallery. They were followed by the founding of the families Pandolfini, Salviati, Pannocchieschi, della Gherardesca, Bartolini Salimbeni, Peruzzi, Mazzei, Venerosi Pesciolini, and more. Some of these homes are true palaces, like that of the Corsini on the banks of the Arno with its prestigious collection of antique paintings, or the Palazzo Capponi on the street with the same name, with its important historical archives and venerable library.

Florence remained closed within its framework of stone, governed by foreign princes and a wealthy crested oligarchy, and enjoying a powerful economy, until the 19th century, when the Napoleonic wind also inspired Italy to begin its tortuous path toward national unity. Tuscany has been replete with Napoleonites, who have been quite welcome in society, but have been replaced later on by a well-educated English and American gentry, who with their artistic ambitions and peaceful intentions even showed their sympathies for Garibaldi and Mazzini, the leaders of the Italian national movement *Risorgimento*. The large palaces had always leased apartments to noble and idealistic English speakers, but now some of the newly arrived were businessmen in search of antiquities or real estate investments to launch on the international market. The Anglophones specialized in reconstructing medieval castles, Medici villas, and city palaces in their own image, and thus the old façades found themselves enriched with Neo-Gothic lunettes of forged iron with obligatory curls.

When Florence was appointed the capital of the young united Italy, previously far-flung ministerial offices arrived, along with the destruction and redesign of a good part of the more populous and essentially Florentine districts. The Second World War and Nazi occupation led to bombing and destruction of a precious slice of the Arno embankments and the historic palaces of the central city. In order to find the ancient soul of Florence beneath the crust of renovations and speculative building, it was necessary to become intimate with the city's oldest families, those who had the knowledge to preserve or recreate the historic heritage of this grand city. They are the fulcrum of the photographic pursuit that illustrates this volume.

Marco Fini

Il lusso toscano

Il lusso toscano non è ostentazione di ricchezza, esibizione di sé. Chi visita per la prima volta le città grandi o piccole di Toscana, a partire da Firenze, rimane colpito dalla strettezza delle strade: i palazzi più importanti, con le loro architetture e i loro stemmi, non sono praticamente visibili se non di scorcio, col naso in su. Come, del resto, molti dei più noti cicli di affreschi dipinti a grandi altezze, su cupole e pareti interne di palazzi e cattedrali. Si può pensare a un'ignoranza tecnica, si possono accusare di snobismo artisti e committenti? No, la ragione è di sostanza. I toscani ricchi e potenti, i fiorentini, i senesi, i pisani, i volterrani (soprattutto quelli delle origini), vogliono "essere" più che "apparire". La scelta della pietra come materia prima degli edifici pubblici e privati risponde a questa esigenza di peso specifico, qualità intrinseca. Firenze, Siena, Arezzo sono città di pietra, ed è la pietra a fare da cornice anche alle più preziose facciate in marmo.

La storia del singolare "lusso" toscano si legge bene nella storia della società in cammino secolare verso la modernità urbana. A partire dai villaggi originari, quasi sempre romani e in qualche caso etruschi, le città nascono come fortezze ricche di torri, abitate da principi guerrieri, circondate da grappoli di case "di servizio" per il popolo minuto. Le torri, col loro sviluppo verticale e gli ingombranti apparati militari, concedono ben poco alle ostentazioni di ricchezza, così come i muniti castelli delle campagne. Ma è proprio dal contado che, alle soglie del Trecento, "la gente nova", come la chiamava con disprezzo Dante, si riversa a Firenze, a impiantare commerci e traffici, fabbriche e banche. Le famiglie si nobilitano rapidamente con in pugno una moneta che diventa il riferimento di tutta l'economia e finanza dell'Europa in espansione. I fiorentini inventano, oltre alla cambiale, anche il palazzo, cassaforte di potenza materiale e deposito, discreto, di grandi giacimenti culturali. Questo nuovo popolo grasso produce artigiani e artisti di ogni tipo, architetti, scultori, pittori, bronzisti, marmisti, falegnami. Tra Quattro e Cinquecento lavorano a Firenze a progettare e riempire delle loro opere chiese e palazzi dei nuovi e vecchi ricchi, Arnolfo di Cambio e Brunelleschi, Michelangelo e Leonardo, le punte di un *made in Tuscany*, che domina la scena internazionale per almeno tre secoli. È questo il lusso fiorentino e toscano.

I primi palazzi del rinnovamento rinascimentale a Firenze si intitolano ai Medici, Rucellai, Pitti, Pazzi, Antinori, Strozzi e Gondi. Al fasto degli arredi è sempre congiunto il "punto d'onore" della grande quadreria, delle collezioni di sculture e oggetti d'arte, dei parchi e giardini botanici. Seguono a ruota le famiglie fondanti, i Pandolfini, i Salviati, i Pannocchieschi, i della Gherardesca, i Bartolini Salimbeni, i Peruzzi, i Mazzei, i Venerosi Pesciolini e così via. Alcuni di questi palazzi sono vere e proprie regge come quello dei Corsini sul Lungarno con la sua prestigiosa collezione di quadri antichi o il palazzo Capponi dell'omonima strada con archivi di importanza storica e una biblioteca venerabile e venerata da sempre.

Firenze è rimasta chiusa nelle sue armature di pietra, governata da principi stranieri e da una oligarchia ricca di stemmi e potenza economica fino all'Ottocento, quando il vento napoleonico ha investito anche l'Italia, avviata nel tormentato cammino verso l'unità nazionale. La Toscana si è riempita di napoleonici, ben accetti in società, a cui succedono gentiluomini e gentildonne inglesi e americane di buone lettere, artistiche ambizioni, intendimenti pacifisti e che dimostrano perfino simpatie garibaldine e mazziniane. I grandi palazzi hanno sempre affittato appartamenti a nobili o idealisti anglofoni; ora alcuni dei nuovi arrivati sono mercanti in cerca di antiquariato da lanciare sui mercati internazionali o di buoni investimenti immobiliari. Gli anglofoni hanno una specialità: ricostruiscono castelli medievali, ville medicee, palazzi di città a loro immagine e somiglianza. Così si vedono le vecchie facciate arricchirsi di lunette neogotiche, di ferri battuti con qualche ricciolo in più del dovuto.

Quando Firenze diventa la capitale della giovane Italia unita, arrivano oltre agli uffici ministeriali, gli sventramenti e il ridisegno di una buona parte dei quartieri più popolari e più fiorentini. La seconda guerra mondiale e l'occupazione nazista cancellano con le bombe una fetta preziosa dei lungarni e dei palazzi storici del centro. Per ritrovare l'anima antica di Firenze, sotto la crosta dei rifacimenti in stile o la pura edilizia di speculazione, bisogna andare a violare la privacy delle più vecchie famiglie cittadine, di quelle che hanno saputo conservare o ricreare il patrimonio storico della città. Sono loro il fulcro della ricerca fotografica che illustra questo volume.

Marco Fini

Der Toskanische Luxus

Der toskanische Luxus dient nicht der Zurschaustellung von Reichtum um seiner selbst willen. Wer von Florenz aus zum ersten Mal die Städte der Toskana besucht, zeigt sich fasziniert von den engen Straßen: Architektur und Wappenschmuck der bedeutenden Palazzi lassen sich nur perspektivisch verkürzt betrachten, indem man den Blick hebt. Das gilt auch für viele der bekanntesten Freskenzyklen, die sich in Kuppeln oder an Innenwänden von Palästen und Kathedralen in großer Höhe befinden. Ist dies auf einen Mangel an technischer Kenntnis zurückzuführen? Oder kann man die Künstler und Auftraggeber des Snobismus beschuldigen? Nein, die Ursache liegt vielmehr darin begründet, dass die reichen und mächtigen Toskaner (besonders die alteingesessenen), ob in Florenz, Siena, Pisa oder Volterra, mehr nach dem „Sein" als nach dem „Schein" streben. Die Wahl des Steins als wichtigsten Rohstoff für den Bau öffentlicher und privater Gebäude wird diesem Anspruch, der besonderes Gewicht auf Qualität legt, gerecht. Florenz, Siena und Arezzo sind Städte aus Stein, ein Material, das selbst den kostbarsten Marmorfassaden als Rahmen dient.

Die Entwicklung des außergewöhnlichen toskanischen Luxus lässt sich anhand der Gesellschaftsgeschichte im Verlauf der Jahrhunderte bis zur modernen Stadt anschaulich nachvollziehen. Ausgehend von den frühen Siedlungen, die fast immer römischen, in einigen Fällen etruskischen Ursprungs sind, entstehen die Städte als turmreiche Festungen, die von streitbaren Fürsten bewohnt werden. Umgeben sind die Wohntürme von kleinen Wirtschaftsgebäuden, die dem *popolo minuto*, dem einfachen Volk dienen. Mit ihrer vertikalen Ausrichtung und ihrer umfangreichen militärischen Ausstattung sind die Türme für die Zurschaustellung von Reichtum wenig geeignet, was auch für die befestigten Landsitze gilt. Ausgerechnet aus dem Umland aber strömt an der Schwelle des 14. Jahrhunderts die „gente nova" (neues Volk), wie Dante sie geringschätzig nannte, nach Florenz, um dort Handel zu treiben oder Geschäfte, Werkstätten oder Banken aufzubauen. Die Familien steigen schnell auf und gelangen zu Wohlstand. Symbol für diesen neuen Wohlstand wird eine Währung, an der sich das gesamte Wirtschafts- und Finanzwesen des expandierenden Europas orientiert, der Goldflorin. Neben dem Wechsel erfinden die Florentiner auch den Palazzo. Er ist Sinnbild materieller Macht und unauffälliges Zentrum großer kultureller Schätze. Das neue Großbürgertum beschäftigt Handwerker und Künstler aller Art: Architekten, Bildhauer, Maler, Bronzegießer, Marmorschleifer und Tischler. Zwischen dem 15. und 16. Jahrhundert sind in Florenz Arnolfo di Cambio, Brunelleschi, Michelangelo und Leonardo tätig, um im Auftrag von Alt- und Neureichen Kirchen und Paläste zu planen und mit ihren Werken auszuschmücken. Sie gelten als Aushängeschilder des *Made in Tuscany*, das für mindestens drei Jahrhunderte in Europa den Ton angeben wird. Dies ist es, was den florentinischen und toskanischen Luxus ausmacht.

Die ersten Palazzi, die im Geiste der Erneuerung der Renaissance entstehen, sind mit den Namen der Medici, Rucellai, Pitti, Pazzi, Antinori, Strozzi und Gondi untrennbar verknüpft. Zur prächtigen Ausstattung gehören immer prestigeträchtige Glanzpunkte wie eine große Gemäldegalerie, Sammlungen von Skulpturen und Kunstgegenständen, Parkanlagen und botanische Gärten. Der alteingesesssene Adel der Pandolfini, Salviati, Pannocchieschi, della Gherardesca, Bartolini Salimbeni, Peruzzi, Mazzei, Venerosi Pesciolini usw. folgt diesem Beispiel. Einige ihrer Palazzi sind regelrechte Königspaläste, so der Palazzo Corsini an der Arnopromenade mit seiner namhaften Sammlung alter Gemälde oder der Palazzo Capponi in der gleichnamigen Straße mit seinen historisch bedeutsamen Archiven und seiner ehrwürdigen, seit jeher hochgeschätzten Bibliothek.

Florenz bewahrte sich seinen steinernen Schutzmantel und wurde bis ins 19. Jahrhundert von fremden Herrschern und einer traditionsreichen und wirtschaftlich mächtigen Oligarchie regiert, als dann die napoleonische Ära auch Italien erreichte und dessen schwierigen Weg zur nationalen Einheit in Gang brachte. Die Toskana füllt sich mit Anhängern Napoleons, die zwar in der Gesellschaft willkommen sind, später jedoch von englischen Adligen oder amerikanischen Weltmännern abgelöst wurden, die eine gute Sprachkultur, künstlerische Ambitionen, friedliche Absichten und sogar Sympathien für Garibaldi und Mazzini, die Anführer der italienischen Nationalbewegung *Risorgimento*, mitbringen. Die großen Palazzi boten schon immer Wohnraum für englischsprachige Adlige und Idealisten. Bei einigen der Neuankömmlinge handelt es sich aber heute vielmehr um Händler, die auf der Suche nach kostbaren Antiquitäten oder guten Immobilieninvestitionen sind, um sie auf den internationalen Markt zu verkaufen. Manche von ihnen haben sich darauf spezialisiert, mittelalterliche Burgen, Medicivillen oder Stadtpaläste nach ihrem Geschmack und eigenen Vorbildern umzugestalten. Auf diese Weise werden die alten Fassaden mit neugotischen Lünetten und schmiedeeisernen, über Gebühr verzierten Elementen bereichert.

Als Florenz Hauptstadt des jungen vereinigten Italiens wird, halten nicht nur die Ministerialbüros Einzug in die Stadt, es kommt auch zum Abriss und zur Neuplanung großer Teile der ursprünglichsten und florentinischsten Viertel. Durch die Bomben des Zweiten Weltkrieges und die nationalsozialistische Besatzung wird ein kostbarer Teil der Arnopromenade und der historischen Palazzi des Zentrums ausgelöscht. Um den alten Geist von Florenz wiederzuentdecken, muss man hinter die Kulissen des vermeintlich stilgetreuen Wiederaufbaus oder der Spekulationsbauten schauen. Dies gelingt, indem man in die Privatsphäre der ältesten städtischen Familien eindringt, die das historische Erbe der Stadt bewahren oder neu begründen konnten. Sie bilden den Mittelpunkt der fotografischen Bestandsaufnahme, die dieses Buch illustriert.

Marco Fini

Le luxe toscan

Le luxe toscan n'est ni une ostentation de richesse, ni une auto-exhibition. Ceux qui visitent pour la première fois les villes de Toscane, grandes ou petites, à commencer par Florence, sont frappés par l'étroitesse des rues : les palais les plus importants, caractérisés par leurs architectures et leurs armoiries, ne sont pratiquement pas visibles, sinon en perspective, le nez levé vers le ciel, tout comme d'ailleurs nombre des plus célèbres représentations de fresques peintes à une grande hauteur sur les coupoles et les murs intérieurs des palais et des cathédrales. Pouvons-nous songer à une ignorance technique ? Pouvons-nous accuser de snobisme artistes et commettants ? Non, car la substance en est la raison. Les Toscans riches et puissants, les Florentins, les Siennois, les Pisans et les habitants de Volterra (notamment ceux des origines) veulent « être » et non « apparaître ». Le choix de la pierre comme matière première des édifices publics et privés répond à cette exigence de poids spécifique, une qualité intrinsèque. Florence, Sienne et Arezzo sont des villes en pierre, celle-ci servant également de toile de fond aux façades en marbre les plus raffinées.

L'histoire du singulier « luxe » toscan se profile clairement au travers de l'histoire de la société en route depuis des siècles vers la modernité urbaine. À partir des premiers villages, presque tous romains et parfois étrusques, les villes apparaissent sous forme de forteresses munies de tours, habitées par des princes guerriers et entourées de groupements de maisons « de fonction » pour le menu peuple. Les tours, avec leur verticalité et leurs encombrants apparats militaires, accordent bien peu de place aux ostentations de richesse, tout comme d'ailleurs les châteaux forts des campagnes. Toutefois, c'est bien en provenance de ces dernières qu'au début du XIVe siècle, « la gente nova », comme la désignait avec mépris Dante, se répand à Florence pour y établir commerces et échanges, usines et banques. Les familles s'ennoblissent rapidement grâce à une monnaie qui devient le point de repère de toute l'économie et la finance d'une Europe en expansion. Outre la lettre de change, les Florentins donnent également naissance au *palazzo*, coffre-fort de puissance matérielle et discret dépôt de grands gisements culturels. Cette nouvelle grosse bourgeoisie produit des artisans et des artistes en tous genres : architectes, sculpteurs, peintres, bronzeurs, marbriers et menuisiers. À Florence, entre le XVe et le XVIe siècles, Arnolfo di Cambio et Brunelleschi, Michelangelo et Leonardo — les représentants d'un *made in Tuscany* qui domine la scène internationale pendant trois siècles au moins — travaillent à réaliser et à remplir de leurs œuvres les églises et les palais des nouveaux et anciens riches. C'est cela le luxe florentin et toscan.

À Florence, aux premiers palais caractérisés par un renouveau du style Renaissance est donné le nom des Medici, Rucellai, Pitti, Pazzi, Antinori, Strozzi et Gondi. Le faste des décorations est toujours associé à la splendeur d'une grande galerie de tableaux, des collections de sculptures et d'objets d'art, des parcs et des jardins botaniques. Puis, se succèdent les familles fondatrices Pandolfini, Salviati, Pannocchieschi, della Gherardesca, Bartolini Salimbeni, Peruzzi, Mazzei, Venerosi Pesciolini et ainsi de suite. Certains de ces édifices s'apparentent à de véritables palais royaux comme celui des Corsini sur le quai de l'Arno avec sa prestigieuse collection de peintures antiques ou le Palazzo Capponi, situé dans la rue portant le même nom, avec ses archives d'une importance historique et sa bibliothèque vénérable et vénérée depuis toujours.

Florence est restée enfermée dans ses armatures de pierre, gouvernée par des princes étrangers et une oligarchie riche en blasons et en puissance économique jusqu'au XIXe siècle lorsque le vent napoléonien a soufflé également sur l'Italie qui a commencé son chemin tumultueux vers l'unité nationale. La Toscane s'est remplie des Napoléoniens, bien intégrés dans la société, mais qui vient ensuite remplacés par des nobles anglais et des gentilshommes américains, de culture élevée, que caractérisent leurs ambitions artistiques, leurs intentions pacifistes, voire même leurs sympathies pour Garibaldi ou Mazzini, les grandes figures du mouvement national italien *Risorgimento*. Les grands palais ont toujours loué leurs appartements à des nobles ou des idéalistes anglophones ; quelques-uns des nouveaux venus sont à présent des marchands en quête d'objets d'art ancien à lancer sur les marchés internationaux ou de bons investissements immobiliers. Les anglophones ont une spécialité : ils reconstruisent des châteaux médiévaux, des villas médicéennes et des palais de ville qui les représentent et leur ressemblent. Ainsi, les anciennes façades s'enrichissent de lunettes néogothiques et de fers forgés caractérisés par quelques boucles en surabondance.

Lorsque Florence devient la capitale de la jeune Italie unifiée, outre l'apparition des bureaux ministériels ont lieu les démolitions et la restructuration d'une grande partie des quartiers les plus populaires et les plus florentins. Les bombes de la Seconde Guerre mondiale et de l'occupation nazie anéantissent une précieuse partie des quais de l'Arno et des palais historiques du centre-ville. Afin de retrouver l'âme antique de Florence sous la couche des réfections architecturales ou sous le manteau des objets de spéculation nous nous devons d'aller violer l'intimité des plus anciennes familles florentines, de celles qui ont su conserver ou recréer le patrimoine historique de la ville. Elles se trouvent au cœur même de la recherche photographique qui illustre ce volume.

Marco Fini

El lujo toscano

El lujo toscano no significa ostentación de riqueza ni su exhibición. Quien visita por primera vez las ciudades grandes o pequeñas de Toscana, empezando por Florencia, queda asombrado por la estrechez de sus calles: los edificios más importantes, con su arquitectura y sus blasones, apenas son visibles si no es en escorzo, mirando hacia arriba. Algo parecido ocurre con muchos de los más famosos ciclos de frescos pintados a gran altura, en cúpulas y muros interiores de palacios y catedrales. ¿Se puede pensar en una cuestión de ignorancia técnica, se puede acusar de esnobismo a artistas y a quienes encargaron tales obras? No, la razón es sustancial. Los toscanos ricos y potentados, los florentinos, los sieneses, los pisanos, los volterranos (sobre todo los de época antigua), buscan más la "esencia" que la "apariencia". La elección de la piedra como materia prima de los edificios públicos de particulares responde a esta exigencia de peso específico y de cualidad intrínseca. Florencia, Siena, Arezzo son ciudades de piedra, y ésta sigue constituyendo también el marco de las más preciosas fachadas de mármol.

La historia del singular "lujo" toscano se lee bien en la historia de la sociedad que por la vía secular se encamina a la modernidad urbana. Partiendo de las poblaciones originarias, casi siempre romanas y en algún caso etruscas, las ciudades surgen como fortalezas con abundantes torres, habitadas desde el principio por guerreros y rodeadas por racimos de casas "de servicio" para el pueblo llano. Las torres, con su desarrollo vertical y su embarazoso aparato militar, se prestan bien poco a la ostentación de riqueza, al igual que ocurre con los castillos fortificados dispersos en el ámbito rural. Pero es precisamente del campo de donde a principios del siglo XIV la "gente nueva", como la llamaba desdeñosamente Dante, se dirige a Florencia para establecer comercios y negocios, talleres y bancos. Las familias se ennoblecen rápidamente con el dinero en la mano, y éste se convierte en el referente de toda la economía y las finanzas de una Europa en expansión. Los florentinos inventan, además de la letra de cambio, el *palazzo*, caja fuerte de poder material y depósito, discreto, de grandes fondos culturales. Este nuevo pueblo de burgueses ricos produce artesanos y artistas de toda índole, arquitectos, escultores, pintores, broncistas, marmolistas, carpinteros. Entre los siglos XV y XVI trabajan en Florencia, proyectando y ocupando con sus obras las iglesias y palacios de los ricos nuevos y viejos, Arnolfo di Cambio y Brunelleschi, Miguel Ángel y Leonardo, las figuras señeras de un *made in Tuscany* que domina la escena internacional durante por lo menos tres siglos. Éste es el lujo florentino y toscano.

Los primeros edificios de la innovación renacentista en Florencia llevan el nombre de los Médicis, los Rucellai, los Pitti, los Pazzi, los Antinori, los Strozzi o los Gondi. Al fasto de las decoraciones va siempre unido el "pundonor" de las grandes galerías de cuadros, de las colecciones de esculturas y objetos artísticos, de los parques y jardines botánicos. Les siguen de cerca las familias fundadoras, los Pandolfini, los Salviati, los Pannocchieschi, los della Gherardesca, los Bartolini Salimbeni, los Peruzzi, los Mazzei, los Venerosi Pesciolini y demás. Algunos de estos edificios son verdaderamente palacios regios, como el de los Corsini en el Lungarno, con su prestigiosa colección de cuadros antiguos, o el Palazzo Capponi, en la calle del mismo nombre, con archivos de importancia histórica y una biblioteca venerable y venerada desde siempre.

Florencia se mantuvo cerrada en su armazón pétrea, gobernada por príncipes extranjeros y por una oligarquía rica en blasones y en potencia económica hasta el siglo XIX, cuando los vientos napoleónicos soplaron sobre Italia, que iniciaba su atormentado camino hacia la unidad nacional. Toscana se llenó entonces de partidarios de Napoleón, bien vistos en sociedad, pero sustituidos más tarde por nobles ingleses y gentilhombres americanos, cultos, con ambiciones artísticas, pretensiones pacifistas e incluso con simpatías por Garibaldi y Mazzini, dirigentes del movimiento nacional italiano *Risorgimento*. Los grandes palacios siempre arrendaron apartamentos a nobles o idealistas anglófonos, pese a que alguno de los recién llegados fuera un comerciante en busca de piezas de anticuario para lanzar a los mercados internacionales o a la caza de buenas inversiones inmobiliarias. Los anglófonos se especializan en la reconstrucción de castillos medievales, villas mediceas o edificios en la ciudad a su imagen y semejanza. Así, las viejas fachadas se enriquecen con lunetos neogóticos, hierros forjados con algún bucle más de lo necesario.

Cuando Florencia se convierte en la capital de la joven Italia unida, llegan, con las dependencias ministeriales, las grandes demoliciones y el nuevo trazado de buena parte de los barrios más populares y más florentinos. La Segunda Guerra Mundial y la ocupación nazi suprimen mediante las bombas una franja preciosa de las calles a orillas del Arno y de los edificios históricos del centro. Para recobrar el alma antigua de Florencia, bajo la corteza de las imitaciones estilísticas y los objetos de especulación hay que violar la privacidad de las viejas familias ciudadanas, aquellas que han sabido conservar o recrear el patrimonio histórico de la ciudad. Son ellas el punto de mira de la indagación fotográfica que ilustra este volumen.

Marco Fini

Malenchini

Palazzo Malenchini, Firenze

Though documents attest to the Malenchini's history in Lombardy from the 15th century, their presence in Florence is relatively recent. The family moved to Tuscany in the 1600s, settling in Livorno to promote their grains business in the busy port city. Their success would eventually extend their presence from Livorno to Odessa on the Black Sea. Beyond commerce, the family was active in civic affairs as well. Notably, Vincenzo Malenchini (1813–1881) was a patriot, both fighting for and helping fund the cause for a unified Italy. He was a deputy in six legislatures, and named senator in 1876. Late in his life, he was given a key to the city of Florence to honor his life-long patriotism.

Anche se i Malenchini nascono storicamente già nel XV secolo in Lombardia, la loro presenza a Firenze è relativamente recente. La famiglia si trasferì in Toscana nel XVII secolo, stabilendosi a Livorno per ampliare la propria attività (il commercio di cereali) sfruttando il trafficatissimo porto della città. Il successo li spinse in poco tempo a espandere la propria influenza fino a Odessa, sul Mar Nero. La famiglia, tuttavia, non fu attiva solo dal punto di vista commerciale, ma anche da quello politico. Vincenzo Malenchini (1813–1881), in particolare, fu un grande patriota che combatté per l'unità d'Italia e ne finanziò la causa. Fu deputato per sei legislature e nel 1876 fu nominato senatore. In età avanzata ricevette in dono le chiavi della città di Firenze, in onore di una vita dedicata alla patria.

Zeugnissen zufolge liegen die Ursprünge der Familie Malenchini in der Lombardei des 15. Jahrhunderts, sodass dieses Geschlecht in Florenz noch nicht so lange ansässig ist. Im 17. Jahrhundert übersiedelte die Familie in die Toskana und ließ sich in Livorno nieder, um in dieser geschäftigen Hafenstadt seinen Getreidehandel auszubauen. Der geschäftliche Erfolg der Malenchinis war derart groß, dass sie den Warenverkehr von Livorno bis nach Odessa am Schwarzen Meer ausdehnen konnten. Überdies war die Familie in der Politik tätig. Vor allem Vincenzo Malenchini (1813–1881) galt als Patriot, der nicht nur für ein vereintes Italien kämpfte, sondern diesen Kampf auch mitfinanzierte. Er war Abgeordneter in sechs Legislaturperioden und wurde 1876 zum Senator berufen. Als Belohnung für seinen lebenslangen Patriotismus erhielt er in späten Jahren den Schlüssel zur Stadt Florenz.

Si certains documents attestent la présence des Malenchini en Lombardie à partir du XVe siècle, leur présence à Florence est relativement récente. La famille s'installa en Toscane deux siècles plus tard, à Livourne, pour pratiquer le négoce des céréales dans ce port animé. Le succès de l'entreprise lui valut de s'étendre de Livourne à Odessa sur la mer Noire. La famille ne se limita pas au commerce, mais participa à la vie politique italienne. Vincenzo Malenchini (1813–1881) entre autres fut un ardent partisan de l'unification italienne et l'un de ses soutiens financiers. Il fut élu à la députation à six reprises, puis nommé sénateur en 1876. À la fin de sa vie, il reçut les clés de la ville de Florence en hommage à sa vie de patriotisme.

Aunque ya hay vestigios de la presencia de esta familia en Lombardía en el siglo XV, sus vínculos con Florencia son relativamente recientes. El clan se trasladó a la Toscana en el siglo XVII y se asentó en Livorno para dedicarse al comercio del grano en la ajetreada ciudad portuaria. Con el tiempo, los Malenchini tuvieron tanto éxito que extendieron su presencia desde Livorno hasta la ciudad de Odesa, a orillas del mar Negro. Además de los negocios, la familia cultivó también los asuntos públicos. Cabe destacar a Vincenzo Malenchini (1813–1881), un patriota que ayudó a fundar y luchó por la causa de una Italia unificada. Fue diputado durante seis legislaturas y nombrado senador en 1876. Al final de sus días se le otorgó la llave de la ciudad de Florencia en honor a toda una vida de patriotismo.

Key to the city of Florence that was given to Senator Vincenzo Malenchini. Above the doorway is a coat of arms with elephant, brought to the family by Maria Bastogi who married Pietro Malenchini.

Chiave della città di Firenze, donata al senatore Vincenzo Malenchini. Sopra il vano della porta si trova lo stemma con elefante, portato in matrimonio da Maria Bastogi, moglie di Pietro Malenchini.

Der Schlüssel zur Stadt Florenz, den der Senator Vincenzo Malenchini erhielt. Über dem Türeingang findet sich ein Wappen mit einem Elefanten, das durch die Heirat von Pietro Malenchini mit Maria Bastogi in die Familie gebracht wurde.

Clé de la ville de Florence qui fut donnée au sénateur Vincenzo Malenchini. Au-dessus de la porte, on remarque les armes avec l'éléphant de Maria Bastogi, épouse de Pietro Malenchini.

La llave de la ciudad de Florencia, concedida al senador Vincenzo Malenchini. Sobre la puerta el escudo de armas de Maria Bastogi, con el motivo de un elefante, quien se casara con Pietro Malenchini.

Ballroom with 18th century cityscape frescoes. A doorframe and neo-Renaissance ceiling echo the Renaissance mantle. The table was crafted from a 16th century bench.

Sala da ballo con affreschi del XVIII secolo raffiguranti un panorama cittadino. La cornice della porta e il soffitto neorinascimentale riprendono il camino del Rinascimento. Il tavolo è stato ricavato da una panca del XVI secolo.

Ballsaal, dessen Wände Fresken mit Stadtansichten aus dem 18. Jahrhundert schmücken. Ein Türrahmen und die Neorenaissance-Decke passen ausgezeichnet zum Kaminsims aus der Renaissance. Der Tisch wurde aus einer Bank aus dem 16. Jahrhundert gefertigt.

Salle de bal ornée de fresques du XVIIIe représentant des paysages urbains. L'encadrement de la porte et le plafond néo-Renaissance font écho à la cheminée Renaissance. La table a été réalisée à partir d'un banc XVIe.

Salón de baile con frescos de paisajes urbanos del siglo XVIII. El marco de la puerta y el techo neorrenacentista imitan el estilo renacentista. La mesa fue realizada con un banco del siglo XVI.

The neo-Renaissance style of the palace is the work of Luigi, the son of Pietro Malenchini and Maria Bastogi.

Lo stile neorinascimentale del palazzo si deve a Luigi, figlio di Pietro Malenchini e Maria Bastogi.

Der Neorenaissance-Stil des Palastes ist das Werk Luigi Malenchinis, des Sohnes von Pietro Malenchini und Maria Bastogi.

L'aspect néo-Renaissance du palais est l'œuvre de Luigi, le fils de Pietro Malenchini et de Maria Bastogi.

El estilo neorrenacentista del palacio se debe a Luigi (hijo de Pietro Malenchini y Maria Bastogi).

Palazzo Malenchini lies along the Arno River, at the foot of the *Ponte alle Grazie*. Both palace and bridge have a long history in Florence, belied somewhat by their modern appearances. The bridge, first built in the 13th century, was Florence's longest, and in its early incarnations, housed shops (similar to *Ponte Vecchio* today), and subsequently, chapels. One chapel, which now is located next to the palace, had an image of the Virgin Mary, which was known to bestow miracles on the thankful (giving this "bridge of mercies" its name). The palace meanwhile, displays a Neo-Renaissance façade, brought about by the architect O. Rezzi in 1849. Just a few years earlier, Vittorio Bellini had fashioned the palace's inner garden spaces. The palace was built for the Alberti family in the 15th century, who brought together two family branches within its walls before offering it as a haven to the Duchess of Madrid and her son in 1887. Pietro Malenchini purchased the palace shortly after, and the family has resided there ever since. Modern challenges have arisen for the bridge and palace; both World War II mines and the flood of 1966 necessitated repair.

Palazzo Malenchini sorge sulle rive dell'Arno, ai piedi di Ponte alle Grazie. Entrambi hanno rappresentato un capitolo molto importante della storia di Firenze, anche se il loro attuale aspetto potrebbe non farlo credere. Il ponte, costruito nel XIII secolo, era il più lungo di Firenze e inizialmente incorporava anche diverse botteghe (come l'attuale Ponte Vecchio) e in seguito alcune cappelle. Una in particolare, oggi collocata accanto al palazzo Malenchini, conteneva un'immagine della Madonna che, come vuole la leggenda, concedeva miracoli ai devoti (da qui suo nome). Il palazzo esibisce una facciata neorinascimentale costruita dall'architetto O. Rezzi nel 1849, mentre dell'intervento (realizzato pochissimi anni prima) sugli spazi dei giardini interni dell'edificio si occupò Vittorio Bellini. Il palazzo venne costruito dagli Alberti nel XV secolo e ospitò fra le sue mura due rami della famiglia. In seguito, nel 1887, fu offerto come dimora alla duchessa di Madrid e suo figlio. Pietro Malenchini lo acquistò pochi anni dopo, e da allora la sua famiglia ha sempre abitato l'edificio. Il palazzo e il ponte, in epoca moderna, hanno subito diversi danni che hanno reso indispensabili effettuare degli interventi di ristrutturazione: prima a causa delle mine, nella Seconda Guerra Mondiale, e poi dell'alluvione del 1966.

Der Palazzo Malenchini ist am Arno gelegen, am Ende der Brücke *Ponte alle Grazie*. Sowohl Palast als auch Brücke blicken auf eine lange Geschichte in Florenz zurück, was sich aufgrund ihres modern wirkenden Äußeren allerdings nicht sofort erkennen lässt. Die Brücke, die erstmalig im 13. Jahrhundert errichtet wurde, war ursprünglich die längste der Stadt und wie der *Ponte Vecchio* von Läden und später auch Kapellen gesäumt. Eine dieser Kapellen, die sich heute neben dem Palast befindet, beherbergte ein Bildnis der Jungfrau Maria, das der Legende zufolge an den Dankbaren Wunder vollbrachte (deshalb auch der Name der Brücke). Den Palast hingegen ziert eine Fassade im Stil der Neorenaissance, die 1849 von dem Architekten O. Rezzi errichtet wurde. Nur wenige Jahre zuvor hatte Vittorio Bellini den Garten im Inneren des Palazzo angelegt. Der Palast wurde ursprünglich im 15. Jahrhundert für das Geschlecht der Alberti erbaut, das zwei Linien ihrer Familie darin beherbergte, ehe dieser 1887 der Herzogin von Madrid und ihrem Sohn als Zufluchtsort offeriert wurde. Kurz darauf erwarb Pietro Malenchini das Gebäude, dessen Familie seitdem hier lebt. Die Brücke und der Palazzo mussten sich übrigens vielfach den Herausforderungen unserer modernen Zeit stellen: Sowohl Minen aus dem Zweiten Weltkrieg als auch die Flut von 1966 machten im Laufe der Jahre zahlreiche Reparaturen notwendig.

Le palais Malenchini, situé sur les rives de l'Arno, jouxte le *Ponte alle Grazie*. Le palais tout comme le pont ont une longue histoire, que leur aspect actuel dément quelque peu. Édifié au XIIIe siècle, le pont était le plus long de Florence, et, à ses débuts, couvert de boutiques (comme le *Ponte Vecchio* aujourd'hui), puis de chapelles. L'une de ces chapelles, qui est désormais placée près du palais, possédait une image de la Vierge Marie qui avait la réputation d'accomplir des miracles pour les fidèles reconnaissants (d'où le nom de « pont des mercis »). Quant au palais, il arbore une façade néo-Renaissance, réalisée par l'architecte O. Rezzi en 1849. Juste quelques années auparavant, Vittorio Bellini avait donné un nouveau visage au parc. La famille Alberti avait fait élever le palais au XVe siècle et deux branches s'y étaient installées. En 1887, la duchesse de Madrid et son fils y trouvèrent refuge. Pietro Malenchini acheta le palais peu de temps après et sa famille l'occupe toujours. Le palais et le pont ont durement souffert au siècle dernier, entre les mines de la Deuxième Guerre mondiale et les inondations de 1966, qui ont imposé des réparations.

El palacio Malenchini se encuentra en la vera del río Arno, a los pies del *Ponte alle Grazie*. Ambas construcciones tienen una larga historia en Florencia, aunque en cierta forma su moderno aspecto parezca desmentirlo. El puente, construido en el siglo XIII, era el más largo de Florencia y en sus orígenes acogía numerosos comercios (al igual que el *Ponte Vecchio* hoy en día) y, por tanto, también capillas. Una de ellas, hoy en día muy próxima al palacio, contiene una imagen de la Virgen María conocida por otorgar milagros o "gracias" (de ahí el nombre del puente). Por otro lado, el palacio luce una fachada neorrenacentista concebida por el arquitecto O. Rezzi en 1849. Sólo unos pocos años antes, Vittorio Bellini había acondicionado los jardines interiores del edificio. El palacio fue construido en el siglo XV por la familia Alberti, que entre sus muros unió dos ramas del clan, antes de ofrecérselo como refugio a la duquesa de Madrid y su hijo en 1887. Pietro Malenchini adquirió poco después la construcción, en la que su familia ha residido desde entonces. Tanto el puente como el palacio han tenido que hacer frente a retos modernos; las minas de la Segunda Guerra Mundial y la riada de 1966 hicieron necesarias varias restauraciones.

The family's historic alpine home area, Val Malenco, is memorialized in the coat of arms with its figures of an apple tree and a slope. A bench from a palace in Parma originally belonged to Raimonda Ferrari Pelati, the grandmother of Luigi Malenchini.

Lo stemma famigliare, con un melo e un'altura, ricorda la storica dimora alpina della famiglia, in Val Malenco. Una panca da un palazzo di Parma, proveniente da Raimonda Ferrari Pelati, nonna di Luigi Malenchini.

Die historische Heimat der Familie, das alpine Val Malenco, spiegelt sich noch im Wappen wider – durch einen Apfelbaum und einen Berghang. Die Bank aus einem Palast in Parma gehörte Raimonda Ferrari Pelati, der Großmutter Luigi Malenchinis.

La région historique de la famille, Val Malenco, dans les Alpes, est évoquée sur le blason par un pommier et une pente. Le banc provenant d'un palais de Parme a été apporté par Raimonda Ferrari Pelati, la grand-mère de Luigi Malenchini.

El origen alpino de la familia, oriunda de Val Malenco, se recuerda en el escudo de armas con un manzano y una pendiente. Banco de un palacio de Parma perteneciente a Raimonda Ferrari Pelati, abuela de Luigi Malenchini.

Ginori

Castello Ginori di Querceto, Ponteginori
Palazzo Ginori, Firenze

The Florentine Palazzo Ginori, on its eponymous Via dei Ginori, was created by uniting existing buildings with a continuous façade between 1516 and 1520 by Baccio d'Agnolo. The Ginori family is renowned not only for its participation in Florentine governance and patronage throughout the centuries of inhabiting this esteemed address, but also for pioneering one of the three hard-paste porcelain companies in Europe (Meissen is another famous example of this style). In 1737, Marchese Carlo Ginori founded the Ginori porcelain company on one of his country properties, Villa Buondelmonti, just outside of Florence, in Doccia. The company was sold by the Ginori family in 1896, and continues production of fine porcelain today under the name Richard Ginori. Though the Ginori name is still linked with fine porcelain, the Ginori Lisci family has turned its attention to wine-making on the Querceto estate, on Tuscany's seacoast of Maremma.

Il Palazzo Ginori di Firenze, situato nell'omonima Via dei Ginori, ebbe origine tra il 1516 e il 1520 dall'unione di alcuni edifici preesistenti per mezzo di una facciata comune, opera di Baccio d'Agnolo. Il lustro della famiglia Ginori, che abitò in questa celebre dimora per diversi secoli, non si deve unicamente alla sua attiva partecipazione alla vita e alla politica della città, ma anche alla fondazione di una delle tre industrie produttrici di porcellana a pasta dura in Europa (tra le quali la famosa Meissen). Nel 1737 il marchese Carlo Ginori fondò la manifattura Ginori in una delle sue tenute di campagna, Villa Buondelmonti a Doccia, nei pressi di Firenze. L'azienda fu venduta dai Ginori nel 1896, ma proseguì l'attività sotto il marchio Richard Ginori, con il quale è conosciuta ancora oggi. Sebbene il suo nome sia rimasto legato alle porcellane di alta qualità, la famiglia Ginori Lisci attualmente si occupa di produzione vinicola nel castello di Querceto, nella Maremma toscana.

Der Palazzo Ginori, der sich in der gleichnamigen Via dei Ginori in Florenz befindet, entstand zwischen 1516 und 1520 durch die Zusammenführung bereits existierender Gebäude. Diese erhielten eine einheitliche Gesamtfassade, die von Baccio d'Agnolo stammt. Die Familie Ginori bewohnt seit Jahrhunderten diese angesehene Adresse, und ebenso lang macht sie ihren Einfluss in der Florentiner Herrschaftsschicht und in ihrer Funktion als Kunstmäzene geltend. Vor allem aber sind die Ginoris für ihre Pionierleistung als Gründer einer der drei europäischen Hartporzellanmanufakturen bekannt (eine weitere ist die Meißener Manufaktur). 1737 errichtete der Marchese Carlo Ginori die Manufaktur auf einem seiner Landsitze, der Villa Buondelmonti, die etwas außerhalb von Florenz in Doccia liegt. Die Firma wurde 1896 von den Ginoris verkauft. Heutzutage wird das feine Porzellan unter dem Namen Richard Ginori produziert. Auch wenn der Name Ginori weiterhin mit Porzellan in Verbindung gebracht wird, hat sich die Familie Ginori Lisci inzwischen auf dem Gut Querceto an der Maremma-Küste ganz und gar der Weinproduktion zugewandt.

Baccio d'Agnolo édifia le palais florentin des Ginori, situé sur l'éponyme via dei Ginori, en réunissant des bâtiments existants derrière une façade continue, entre 1516 et 1520. La famille Ginori doit sa notoriété à sa participation à la vie politique de Florence et à son mécénat au cours des siècles passés à cette adresse prestigieuse, mais aussi pour avoir lancé l'une des trois fabriques de porcelaine à pâte dure en Europe (Meissen étant un autre exemple connu de ce genre). En 1737, le marquis Carlo Ginori fonda la fabrique Ginori dans l'une de ses propriétés à la campagne, la Villa Buondelmonti, à Doccia, juste aux abords de Florence. Les Ginori vendirent en 1896 l'entreprise qui a poursuivi son activité sous le nom de Richard Ginori jusqu'à nos jours. Si le nom des Ginori reste lié à la belle porcelaine, les Ginori Lisci se consacrent désormais à la viticulture sur leur domaine de Querceto, sur le littoral de la Maremme.

El florentino palacio Ginori, situado en la epónima Via dei Ginori, fue construido entre los años 1516 y 1520 por Baccio d'Agnolo, que unió los edificios preexistentes recubriéndolos con una fachada común. El renombre de la familia Ginori se debe no sólo a su participación en el gobierno y la política de Florencia durante todos los siglos que ha habitado esta noble residencia, sino también a la posesión de una de las tres empresas pioneras de Europa en la fabricación de porcelana de pasta dura (Meissen es otro famoso ejemplo de este estilo). En 1737, Marchese Carlo Ginori fundó la compañía Ginori en una de sus propiedades rústicas, Villa Buondelmonti, situada en Doccia a las afueras de Florencia. En 1896, la familia vendió la empresa, que continuó la producción bajo la marca de Richard Ginori. Aunque el apellido del clan aún sigue ligado así a la porcelana fina, los Ginori Lisci se dedican actualmente a la vitivinicultura en su estancia de Querceto, sita en las tierras litorales toscanas de Maremma.

The Querceto Castle has been valued for its strategic location and valuable assets throughout its nearly thousand-year history. The map on the back of the wine cellar shows the Querceto estate.

Nella sua storia quasi millenaria il castello di Querceto è sempre stato apprezzato per la posizione strategica e le preziose risorse. La mappa sulla parete di fondo della cantina mostra la tenuta di Querceto.

Die Burg Querceto wird seit beinahe eintausend Jahren für ihre strategisch ausgezeichnete Lage und ihre wertvollen Güter geschätzt. Die Karte an der Rückwand des Weinkellers zeigt das gesamte Anwesen von Querceto.

Le château de Querceto a été apprécié pour sa situation stratégique et ses magnifiques possessions tout au long de son histoire presque millénaire. Le plan sur le mur arrière des chais représente la propriété de Querceto.

El castillo Querceto ha sido siempre apreciado por su situación estratégica y sus valiosas propiedades durante sus casi mil años de historia. El plano al fondo de la bodega muestra la estancia Querceto.

Bedroom for *Carlo Ginori's 1875 marriage to Maria Luisa Álvarez Calderón. All the furniture was made specifically for the room by ebonist Luigi Frullini.*

Camera da letto *per il matrimonio di Carlo Ginori e Maria Luisa Álvarez Calderón nel 1875. I mobili furono creati appositamente per la stanza dall'ebanista Luigi Frullini.*

Schlafgemach für *Carlo Ginoris Hochzeit mit Maria Luisa Álvarez Calderón im Jahr 1875. Die gesamten Möbel wurden von dem Ebenisten Luigi Frullini extra für dieses Zimmer angefertigt.*

Chambre décorée *en 1875 pour le mariage de Carlo Ginori avec Maria Luisa Álvarez Calderón. L'ébéniste Luigi Frullini réalisa tout le mobilier spécialement pour cette pièce.*

Alcoba para el *enlace de Carlo Ginori en 1875 con Maria Luisa Álvarez Calderón. Todos los muebles fueron fabricados especialmente para el dormitorio por el ebanista Luigi Frullini.*

Palazzo Ginori has been shaped by the generations of family that have celebrated life events in its rooms. Much of its décor and adornments have been created in honor of family weddings and events, and the palace has been painstakingly restored and updated throughout its five hundred year history. A room with a floor-to-ceiling stucco curtain ornamented with figures was created for a 17ᵗʰ century wedding, and an ornate bedroom of hand-carved furniture was crafted for another family wedding in the 19ᵗʰ century. In addition, the ballroom was redecorated in 1880, using Flemish tapestries and ornate early-Venetian chandeliers. Restructuring has not been limited to the inside of the palace—in fact, Lorenzo Ginori Lisci's marriage to Ottavia Strozzi in 1846 was the inspiration to pave the courtyard in marble and enclose it with a cast iron and glass skylight. In the same century, the architect Gaetano Baccani was instructed to lower the height of the Ginori houses across the street to allow light to flow into the street, and to reach the interior of the palace.

Il Palazzo Ginori è stato continuamente rimodellato di generazione in generazione, spesso in occasione delle numerose feste familiari tenutesi all'interno delle sue stanze. Gran parte degli arredi e delle decorazioni, infatti, sono stati realizzati per celebrare matrimoni o altri eventi sociali e il palazzo non ha mai cessato di essere accuratamente restaurato e rimodernato nel corso di tutti i suoi cinquecento anni di esistenza. Si deve a una festa di nozze avvenuta nel XVII secolo, per esempio, la creazione di una stanza con una tenda di stucco arricchita di figure ornamentali che va dal pavimento al soffitto, mentre per un altro matrimonio di famiglia avvenuto nel XIX secolo fu commissionata una sontuosa camera da letto con mobili intagliati a mano. Gli arredi del salone da ballo, tra cui figurano arazzi fiamminghi e sfarzosi candelieri realizzati in stile veneziano antico, risalgono invece al 1880. I rimaneggiamenti non hanno però interessato esclusivamente gli interni del palazzo. Nel 1846, infatti, le nozze tra Lorenzo Ginori Lisci e Ottavia Strozzi rappresentarono l'occasione per lastricare il cortile in marmo e coprirlo con un lucernario in vetro e ghisa. Sempre nel XIX secolo, l'architetto Gaetano Baccani fu incaricato di abbassare le case di fronte al palazzo, anch'esse dei Ginori, per permettere alla luce solare di illuminare la via e raggiungere le sale interne.

Der Palazzo Ginori trägt die Handschrift vieler Generationen, die hier nicht nur gelebt, sondern auch zahlreiche Feste ausgerichtet haben. Üppige Ausschmückungen und Zierrat wurden für festliche Anlässe wie Hochzeiten oder Ähnliches dem Gebäude hinzugefügt, das während seiner 500-jährigen Geschichte immer wieder sorgfältigst renoviert und modernisiert wurde. So wurde ein Raum mit einer Stuckverzierung, die wie ein Vorhang vom Boden bis zur Decke reicht und mit Figuren versehen ist, für eine Hochzeit im 17. Jahrhundert ausgestattet. Für eine weitere Hochzeit im 19. Jahrhundert wurde eines der Schlafzimmer kunstvoll mit handgeschnitztem Mobiliar ausgestattet. Zudem ließ man 1880 den Ballsaal renovieren und mit flämischen Wandteppichen sowie reich verzierten frühvenezianischen Kronleuchtern ausstatten. Renovierungsarbeiten wurden jedoch nicht nur im Inneren des Palastes ausgeführt. So führte die Heirat von Lorenzo Ginori Lisci und Ottavia Strozzi im Jahr 1846 dazu, dass man den Innenhof mit Marmor auskleidete und mit einem Dach aus Gusseisen und Glas überfing. Im gleichen Jahrhundert wurde der Architekt Gaetano Baccani beauftragt, die Höhe der Ginori-Häuser auf der gegenüberliegenden Straßenseite zu verringern, damit mehr Licht in die Straße und somit auch in das Innere des Palastes fallen konnte.

Les générations qui ont célébré les grands événements familiaux dans le palais Ginori lui ont donné son visage actuel. Une grande partie de son décor et de ses ornements ont été créés en l'honneur de mariages et d'événements, ce qui n'a pas empêché ses habitants de le rénover avec soin et de le remettre au goût du jour tout au long de ses 500 ans d'existence. Ainsi, un rideau historié en stuc allant du plafond au sol fut imaginé pour un mariage au XVIIᵉ siècle et une somptueuse chambre au mobilier sculpté rappelle une autre union, célébrée au XIXᵉ. Par ailleurs, la salle de bal fut redécorée en 1880, avec des tapisseries flamandes et de superbes lustres anciens de Venise. Les restructurations ne se sont pas limitées aux intérieurs. En fait, le mariage de Lorenzo Ginori Lisci et d'Ottavia Strozzi en 1846 fut l'occasion de paver de marbre la cour et de la recouvrir d'une verrière en verre et en fonte. Toujours au XIXᵉ, l'architecte Gaetano Baccani fut chargé de réduire la hauteur des maisons Ginori situées de l'autre côté de la rue, afin de laisser plus de lumière atteindre la rue et l'intérieur du palais.

El palacio Ginori se ha ido conformando por las diversas generaciones de la familia que durante siglos han celebrado eventos de su vida en estas estancias. Gran parte de la decoración y los ornamentos fueron encargados con motivo de bodas y otras celebraciones familiares. Y es que a lo largo de sus quinientos años de historia, el palacio ha sido restaurado y modernizado cuidadosamente en varias ocasiones. Así se acondicionó una sala con paredes totalmente recubiertas de estuco con figuras ornamentales para una boda familiar que se celebró en el siglo XVII y se encargó una alcoba con muebles tallados a mano con ocasión de otra boda, esta vez en el siglo XIX. Asimismo en 1880 se redecoró el salón de baile con tapices flamencos, y antiguas y ornamentales lámparas de araña venecianas. Pero las remodelaciones no se limitaron al interior del palacio; de hecho, por motivo de las nupcias de Lorenzo Ginori Lisci con Ottavia Strozzi en 1846, el patio se pavimentó de mármol y se cubrió con una claraboya de cristal y hierro fundido. Ese mismo siglo, el arquitecto Gaetano Baccani recibió el encargo de reducir la altura de las casas Ginori del otro lado de la calle para permitir que entrara la luz hasta el interior del vecino palacio.

*The palazzo's **Sala degli Stucchi** (stucco room) with coat of arms was created for the Ginori–Rucellai wedding of 1699. The Courtyard of the original palace dating from 1516–1520 with corona robbiana.*

***La Sala degli Stucchi**, con stemma, fu creata in occasione del matrimonio Ginori–Rucellai nel 1699. La corte del palazzo originale, del 1516–1520, con la corona robbiana.*

***Der Sala degli Stucchi** (Stuck-Saal) mit dem Wappen wurde für die eheliche Verbindung der Ginori mit den Rucellai 1699 errichtet. Der Innenhof des ursprünglichen Palastes von 1516–1520 mit der Corona Robbiana.*

***La Sala degli Stucchi** (salle des stucs) du palais, avec les armoiries, fut réalisée en l'honneur du mariage Ginori–Rucellai, en 1699. La cour du palais d'origine de 1516–1520, avec la corona robbiana.*

***La Sala degli Stucchi** (Sala de los estucos) con el escudo de armas fue acondicionada para la boda Ginori–Rucellai en 1699. Patio del palacio original de 1516–1520 con corona robbiana.*

Pannocchieschi d'Elci

Palazzo Pannocchieschi d'Elci, Siena

As afternoon shadows lengthen in *Piazza del Campo*, famous setting of Siena's *Palio*, there may be no better vantage point for watching this race than Palazzo Pannocchieschi d'Elci, situated directly above the race's start and end point. Siena's signature colors of black and white adorn the exterior walls of the elegant *palazzo*, testifying to its inextricable connection with Siena's history; its walls once defined the boundary of the city (and its basements house ancient prisons). Indeed, Siena's signature *piazza* took shape in the palace's shadow. It has been the home of the Pannocchieschi d'Elci since the end of the 1700s.

Quando le ombre del pomeriggio si allungano su Piazza del Campo, famosa cornice del Palio di Siena, non esiste miglior punto d'osservazione per assistere alla corsa dei cavalli che il Palazzo Pannocchieschi d'Elci, situato proprio in corrispondenza del punto di partenza e di arrivo della gara. I colori tradizionali di Siena, il bianco e il nero, adornano le pareti esterne di questo elegante palazzo, a testimonianza del suo inscindibile legame con la storia della città; le sue mura un tempo indicavano infatti il confine di Siena (il piano interrato conserva ancora delle antiche prigioni). In effetti, si può dire che la piazza simbolo di Siena sia nata all'ombra di questo palazzo, dimora della famiglia Pannocchieschi d'Elci sin dalla fine del XVIII secolo.

Wenn die Nachmittagssonne langsam schwächer wird und sich lange Schatten auf die *Piazza del Campo* legen, – der berühmten Kulisse für Sienas *Palio* –, gibt es wohl keinen besseren Platz, um dem Rennen zuzuschauen, als den Palazzo Pannocchieschi d'Elci. Er befindet sich nämlich direkt über dem Start beziehungsweise Ziel. Sienas berühmte Farben Schwarz und Weiß schmücken die Außenwände dieses eleganten Palastes und sind Ausdruck für die unentwirrbaren Verknüpfungen mit der Geschichte der Stadt Siena. Die Mauern des *Palazzo* bildeten früher einmal die Stadtgrenze (und in seinen Kellerräumen kann man noch heute uralte Verliese entdecken). Ja, sogar Sienas berühmteste *Piazza* wurde im Schatten dieses Palastes erbaut, der seit dem Ende des 18. Jahrhunderts der Familiensitz der Pannocchieschi d'Elci ist.

Tandis que les ombres s'allongent sur la *Piazza del Campo*, cadre célèbre du *Palio* de Sienne, le palais Pannocchieschi d'Elci, situé directement au-dessus de la ligne de départ et d'arrivée, semble être le meilleur point de vue pour regarder la fameuse course. Les couleurs emblématiques de Sienne, le noir et le blanc, ornent les murs extérieurs de cette élégante demeure, témoignant de ses liens étroits avec l'histoire de la cité ; autrefois, ses murs en marquaient les limites (et les sous-sols abritaient des prisons). En fait, la place qui symbolise la ville a pris forme à l'ombre du palais. Les Pannocchieschi d'Elci y résident depuis la fin du XVIIIe siècle.

Cuando las sombras del atardecer se alargan sobre la *Piazza del Campo*, famoso escenario del *Palio* de Siena, no hay mejor lugar para observar esta carrera de caballos que el palacio Pannocchieschi d'Elci, situado directamente junto al lugar de salida y meta de la competición. Los colores negro y blanco, símbolo de la ciudad de Siena, engalanan las murallas exteriores del elegante *palazzo*, dando así testimonio de su inextricable conexión con la historia de la ciudad; sus muros demarcaron antaño los límites de Siena (y sus sótanos fueron antiguas mazmorras). Por tanto, la emblemática plaza de la ciudad fue conformada a la sombra de este palacio que ha constituido el hogar de los Pannocchieschi d'Elci desde finales del siglo XVIII.

The magnificent palace was substantively updated in 1834 with work from leading architects and artists, including Agostino Fantastici and Alessandro Maffei. It continues to be the home of Cesarina Pannocchieschi d'Elci; her children live in residences here as well. And, though it could be described as a "family home," the *palazzo* maintains its ties to the community. Its vermeil and silver chapel, formerly in the *Duomo* of Siena, is displayed on the day of St. John. In addition, the family doesn't simply have front row seats to the famous *Palio*, but as part of the Selva *contrada* (neighborhood) of Siena, the team has dominated the race many times.

Il maestoso palazzo nel 1834 venne quasi completamente ridefinito a opera di insigni architetti quali Agostino Fantastici e Alessandro Maffei. Nei vari appartamenti vivono ancor oggi Cesarina Pannocchieschi d'Elci e i suoi figli. Pur potendosi definire una "casa di famiglia", il suo legame con la comunità cittadina non è mai venuto meno. La cappella del palazzo, decorata in argento e vermeil (un tempo collocata nel Duomo di Siena), viene aperta al pubblico il giorno di San Giovanni. La famiglia, oltre a poter assistere al famoso Palio da una posizione privilegiata, fa anche parte della contrada Selva che ha spesso dominato la corsa dei cavalli.

Der prächtige Palast wurde 1834 erheblich restauriert und modernisiert, wobei bedeutende Architekten und Künstler mitwirkten, wie zum Beispiel Agostino Fantastici und Alessandro Maffei. Heutzutage leben hier Cesarina Pannocchieschi d'Elci und ihre Kinder, die ihre eigenen Trakte bewohnen. Auch wenn der Palazzo als Familiensitz bezeichnet werden kann, so behält er doch weiterhin seine enge Verbindung zur Stadt. Die mit Silbergold und Silber geschmückte Privatkapelle der Familie, die sich ursprünglich im Dom von Siena befand, ist am Namenstag des Heiligen Johannes für die Öffentlichkeit zugänglich. Außerdem hat die Familie beim berühmten *Palio* nicht nur Plätze in vorderster Reihe, sondern als Teil der Selva *contrada* (Gemeinde) von Siena das Rennen auch schon oft angeführt.

Le magnifique palais fut très remanié en 1834 par des architectes et des artistes de renom, notamment Agostino Fantastici et Alessandro Maffei. Cesarina Pannocchieschi d'Elci y vit toujours, non loin de ses enfants. Et si le palais peut être qualifié de « maison familiale », il maintient ses liens avec la communauté. Le jour de la Saint-Jean, le public peut contempler sa chapelle en vermeil et en argent, qui se trouvait autrefois dans la cathédrale. En outre, la famille ne se contente pas simplement de fauteuils au premier rang lors du *Palio*, mais, puisqu'elle fait partie de la *contrada* (quartier) de la Selva, elle a partagé la victoire à plusieurs reprises.

El magnífico palacio fue profundamente remodelado en 1834 con ayuda de renombrados arquitectos y artistas, entre ellos Agostino Fantastici y Alessandro Maffei. Hoy en día sigue siendo el hogar de Cesarina Pannocchieschi d'Elci, y de sus hijos. A pesar de su carácter de residencia particular, el palacio mantiene sus vínculos con la comunidad: la capilla en tonos bermejos y plateados, anteriormente situada en el *Duomo* de Siena, se abre al público el día de San Juan. Por otro lado, la familia no sólo disfruta de un palco de honor para contemplar el *Palio*, sino que también forma parte de la *contrada* della Selva o barrio de Siena equipo ganador de la carrera en muchas ocasiones.

The Red Salon with painted ceiling by Alessandro Maffei containing the Pannocchieschi d'Elci coat of arms.

Il salone rosso, con il soffitto dipinto da Alessandro Maffei con lo stemma dei Pannocchieschi d'Elci.

Der Rote Salon mit einer von Alessandro Maffei gemalten Decke samt Familienwappen der Pannocchieschi d'Elci.

Le plafond du salon rouge, peint aux armes des Pannocchieschi d'Elci, est l'œuvre d'Alessandro Maffei.

Salón rojo con techos pintados por Alessandro Maffei con el escudo de armas de Pannocchieschi d'Elci.

The **bedroom** (attributed to Fantastici); the palace's façade seen from Siena's Piazza del Campo; and book of marriages, illustrating centuries of the coats of arms of those who have married into the family.

La camera da letto, attribuita a Fantastici, la facciata del palazzo dalla piazza del Campo, e il registro dei matrimoni, con gli stemmi delle casate entrate a far parte per matrimonio della famiglia nel corso dei secoli.

Das Fantastici zugeschriebene Schlafgemach; die Palastfassade von der Piazza del Campo in Siena aus gesehen; sowie ein Hochzeitsbuch mit den Wappen derjenigen, die über die Jahrhunderte in die Familie eingeheiratet haben.

La chambre attribuée à Fantastici, la façade du palais depuis la Piazza del Campo de Sienne et le livre des mariages, illustrant plusieurs siècles d'armoiries de tous les alliés de cette famille.

Alcoba atribuida a Fantastici, fachada del palacio a la plaza del Campo de Siena, y libro de enlaces que ilustra cientos de escudos de armas de todos aquellos que se casaron con miembros de la familia.

These descendants of the Counts of Elci did not make this famous Siena address their home without a struggle, however. The historic home of the family, from 1219, was the hilltop hamlet of Elci—the family's extensive landholdings once included 36 castles and hamlets in Tuscany's seacoast territory extending from Pisa to Grosseto. Attempts by Siena to conquer Elci—to keep rivals from becoming too strong—left the Elci castle in ruin three times before the family relented to joining with Siena, and moving into town.

Per fare di questo famoso indirizzo di Siena la propria residenza, tuttavia, i discendenti dei conti d'Elci dovettero superare diversi ostacoli. La casa natale della famiglia, sin dal 1219, si trovava nel piccolo borgo collinare di Elci (i grandi possedimenti terrieri della famiglia un tempo comprendevano 36 tra castelli e villaggi sparsi sul territorio costiero della Toscana, da Pisa fino a Grosseto). I tentativi di Siena di conquistare Elci, per impedire ai rivali di accumulare un potere eccessivo, causarono per ben tre volte la distruzione del castello d'Elci, dopo di che la famiglia si rassegnò e accettò la sconfitta, trasferendosi in città.

Den Nachfahren der Grafen von Elci gelang es nicht ohne Schwierigkeiten, diese berühmte Adresse in Siena zu ihrem Eigentum zu machen. Der ursprüngliche Wohnsitz der Familie befand sich seit 1219 in dem kleinen Ort Elci, das auf einem Hügel liegt. Zu dem enormen Landbesitz gehörten einmal 36 Schlösser und Dörfer an der toskanischen Küste, von Pisa bis Grosseto gelegen. Siena versuchte Elci zu erobern, um mögliche Feinde gar nicht erst erstarken zu lassen, und ließ die Burg Elci dreimal zerstören, ehe die Familie nachgab, sich Siena anschloss und in die Stadt zog.

Ces descendants des comtes d'Elci n'ont du reste pas conquis cette adresse prestigieuse sans lutte. Le berceau familial depuis 1219 coiffait la colline où se niche le village d'Elci – les vastes possessions territoriales de la famille comprenaient 36 châteaux et villages le long des côtes de la Toscane, de Pise à Grosseto. Les Siennois tentèrent de conquérir Elci, afin d'empêcher leurs rivaux de prendre trop d'importance, et rasèrent le château d'Elci à trois reprises avant que les comtes ne consentent à se rallier à Sienne et à s'y installer.

Sin embargo, los descendientes de los condes de Elci hicieron de esta famosa dirección de Siena su hogar no sin antes pagar un alto precio. La histórica residencia de la familia desde 1219 había sido la estancia de Elci, situada sobre un cerro. Sus vastas propiedades incluían 36 castillos y casonas en las tierras litorales toscanas que se extendían entre Pisa y Grosseto. Los intentos de Siena por conquistar Elci –para evitar que sus rivales se hiciesen demasiado poderosos–, redujeron el castillo de la familia a ruinas en tres ocasiones antes de que el clan consintiera en aliarse con su enemigo y se mudara a la ciudad.

The view toward Siena's most famous square provides an ideal backdrop for a family event. Marina Pannocchieschi d'Elci with a friend, and Viéri celebrating the christening of Marina's daughter Bianca.

La vista sulla piazza più celebre di Siena è uno sfondo d'eccezione per una riunione familiare. Marina Pannocchieschi d'Elci con un'amica e Viéri al ricevimento per il battesimo di Bianca, figlia di Marina.

Der Blick auf den berühmtesten Platz Sienas bildet den perfekten Hintergrund für ein Familienfest. Marina Pannocchieschi d'Elcis mit einer Freundin und Viéri bei der Tauffeier für Bianca, Marinas Tochter.

La vue sur la plus célèbre place de Sienne constitue l'arrière-plan idéal pour une fête de famille. Marina Pannocchieschi d'Elci avec une amie, et Viéri à la réception à l'occasion du baptême de Bianca, la fille de Marina.

La vista de la más famosa plaza de Siena es el telón de fondo perfecto para cualquier evento familiar. Marina Pannocchieschi d'Elci con una amiga, y Viéri celebrando el bautizo de la hija de Marina, Bianca.

Frescobaldi

Palazzo Frescobaldi, Firenze
Castello di Nipozzano, Pelago

The Frescobaldis have been making connections within Florence and around the world for centuries. In their positions of power and prestige, they have forged bonds on behalf of and suffered at the hands of their home city of Florence throughout the ages. In medieval Florence, the Frescobaldi were known as valiant and fierce fighters on behalf of their patria, but also found themselves at odds with the ruling powers over an abusive captain, and unsuccessfully plotted his ouster. Known as the Frescobaldi conspiracy, it ended in beheading and banishment. As progenitors in Florence, 1252 witnessed their call to build *Ponte Santa Trinita* to span the Arno River, and their financial command led to financing several Kings of England and commissioning *Santo Spirito* church. In modern times, they have excelled at creating wine partnerships that extend their influence and prominence across oceans and throughout the wine world.

I Frescobaldi sono divenuti famosi per la fitta rete di conoscenze intessute sia a Firenze che in tutto il mondo. Grazie al potere e al prestigio di cui godevano, per secoli hanno contribuito a forgiare alleanze in nome della propria città, ma allo stesso tempo Firenze è stata per loro anche causa di grandi sofferenze. Nel medioevo i Frescobaldi erano conosciuti come combattenti valorosi e strenui difensori di Firenze, ma si trovarono in aperto contrasto con i governanti della città, allorché pianificarono un fallimentare tentativo di destituzione contro un capitano particolarmente dedito alle sopraffazioni. Questa congiura costò ai Frescobaldi la decapitazione di un membro del casato e l'esilio di alcuni altri. Nel 1252 gli antenati della famiglia organizzarono la costruzione del Ponte Santa Trinita sul fiume Arno, e grazie al loro potere economico finanziarono numerosi sovrani inglesi, nonché la costruzione della Chiesa di Santo Spirito. Più recentemente, i Frescobaldi si sono distinti per le partnership con aziende vinicole straniere che hanno permesso loro di espandersi e trasformare il loro nome in sinonimo di qualità per gli intenditori di vino di tutto il mondo.

Über Jahrhunderte hinweg haben die Frescobaldis ihre Verbindungen in Florenz und in der ganzen Welt ausgebaut. Mit ihrer Macht und ihrem Ansehen knüpften sie für ihre Heimatstadt Florenz viele wichtige Beziehungen, litten aber auch hier und da unter der eisernen Faust dieser Stadt. Im mittelalterlichen Florenz waren die Frescobaldis als tapfere und kühne Kämpfer bekannt, die sich mutig für ihr Vaterland schlugen, auch wenn sie nicht immer zwangsläufig auf der Seite der Macht standen. So versuchten sie zum Beispiel einen willkürlich herrschenden Hauptmann zu stürzen, was ihnen allerdings misslang. Diese wurde als die Frescobaldi-Verschwörung bekannt und führte zu einer Hinrichtung und zu Verbannungen. 1252 ließen die Stammväter des Geschlechts die *Ponte Santa Trinita* über den Arno erbauen, finanzierten später mehrere englische Herrscher und erteilten den Auftrag, die Kirche *Santo Spirito* zu errichten. Auch in jetziger Zeit spielen die Frescobaldis noch immer eine bedeutende Rolle – heutzutage jedoch als Weinproduzenten. Sie genießen großen Einfluss und Anerkennung in der internationalen Weinwelt.

Le nom des Frescobaldi résonne à Florence comme dans le monde entier depuis des siècles. En raison de leur puissance et de leur prestige, leur histoire est indissociable de celle de leur patrie, Florence, pour laquelle ils ont aussi souffert au fil des siècles. Au Moyen Âge, les Frescobaldi étaient connus comme des guerriers vaillants et téméraires, au service de leur patrie, mais ils durent lutter contre un gouvernement tyrannique, qu'ils ne réussirent pas à renverser. La conspiration des Frescobaldi se termina par l'exécution du chef de fil et le bannissement. En 1252, leurs ancêtres firent construire le *Ponte Santa Trinita* qui devait permettre de franchir l'Arno et ces puissants financiers vinrent à l'aide de plusieurs rois d'Angleterre et commanditèrent l'église *Santo Spirito*. À une époque plus récente, ils ont réussi à établir de solides partenariats dans le domaine de la viticulture, qui ont étendu leur influence par-delà les océans et dans tout le monde viticole.

Los Frescobaldi han estado bien relacionados tanto en Florencia como en el resto del mundo durante siglos. En su privilegiada posición de poder y prestigio han forjado alianzas en ayuda de su ciudad natal de Florencia, pero también han sufrido por su causa a lo largo del tiempo. En la Florencia medieval, los Frescobaldi fueron conocidos como valientes y aguerridos guerreros que lucharon por su patria, aunque también se levantaron contra el poder de un abusivo capitán y fracasaron en el complot para derrocarlo. La llamada conspiración de Frescobaldi terminó con una decapitación y penas de destierro. En el año 1252, estos patriarcas florentinos reclamaron la construcción del *Ponte Santa Trinita* para poder cruzar el río Arno; asimismo su poderío económico les permitió financiar a varios reyes ingleses y encargar la iglesia del *Santo Spirito*. En fechas más recientes, los Frescobaldi han creado varias sociedades comerciales vinícolas con las que han ido extendiendo su influencia y prominencia allende los mares, por todo el mundo del vino.

Lamberto and Eleonora Frescobaldi's palazzo residence elegantly balances historic art (della Robbia) with modern masters.

La casa di Lamberto ed Eleonora Frescobaldi, all'interno del palazzo, coniuga arte antica (della Robbia) con maestri moderni in un elegante equilibrio.

Lamberto und Eleonora Frescobaldis Einrichtungsstil im Palazzo verbindet auf elegante Weise alte Kunstwerke (della Robbia) mit modernen Meistern.

Les appartements agencés par Lamberto et Eleonora Frescobaldi dans le palazzo, instaurent un équilibre élégant entre art ancien (della Robbia) et maîtres modernes.

El hogar de Lamberto y Eleonora Frescobaldi en el palacio equilibra de forma elegante el arte histórico (della Robbia) con los maestros modernos.

Bona Frescobaldi is well known for her distinctive hospitality at Palazzo Frescobaldi—here, family and friends have gathered to celebrate the first communion of her granddaughter Leonia.

Bona Frescobaldi è nota per la sua raffinata ospitalità a Palazzo Frescobaldi. Qui un ricevimento per amici e parenti in occasione della Prima Comunione della nipote Leonia.

Bona Frescobaldi ist für ihre besondere Gastfreundlichkeit im Palazzo Frescobaldi berühmt. Die Erstkommunion ihrer Enkelin Leonia wird mit einem Empfang für Freunde und Verwandte gefeiert.

Bona Frescobaldi est connue pour son hospitalité remarquable au Palazzo Frescobaldi – pour fêter la première communion de sa petite-fille Leonia, elle organise une réception pour ses amis et la famille.

Bona Frescobaldi es conocida por su gran hospitalidad en el Palazzo Frescobaldi. La primera comunión de su nieta Leonia celebrada con una recepción de familiares y amigos.

Palazzo Frescobaldi, with its private and intimate view of *Santo Spirito* church, is alive with family. The Frescobaldi heritage lives on here, as ever, reinvigorating the family's continuing history. The Palazzo also teems with the Frescobaldi family business—wine. The family's business philosophy embodies the idea of continually updating, examining methods and traditions of thinking about and engaging in the business, in order to improve and energize it, while respecting the need for continuity with past generations. Lamberto Frescobaldi says, "it is a marathon we are running, and so it is more important to keep going without stopping, rather than being fastest." The Frescobaldi ascribe to the idea that what they have access to—from their treasure trove of history, responsibility and privilege—is theirs to 'use,' rather than own, to be returned, after their own time, for their children and their children's children to use. Eleonora Frescobaldi's perspective of what they will pass to their children is, "giving them wings as well as roots."

A Palazzo Frescobaldi, che gode di una panoramica privata e intima sulla chiesa di *Santo Spirito*, si respira aria di famiglia. L'eredità dei Frescobaldi vive intatta tra le sue mura, ora come un tempo, dando nuova linfa ai secoli di storia del casato. Il Palazzo brulica di attività, legata alla produzione di famiglia: il vino. La filosofia dei Frescobaldi è inseguire un'ideale di rinnovamento continuo, studiando le tecniche e la storia della viticoltura, allo scopo di migliorarla e infonderle sempre nuovo vigore, sempre nel rispetto della continuità con le generazioni passate. Secondo Lamberto Frescobaldi "stiamo correndo una maratona, quindi è più importante andare avanti senza fermarsi anziché cercare di essere i più veloci". L'ideale che inseguono è quello di "mettere a frutto", e non possedere, il patrimonio di storia e conoscenze che derivano dal prestigio e dai privilegi della famiglia, per poterlo consegnare e far utilizzare alle loro generazioni future. Eleonora Frescobaldi spiega così questa eredità da lasciare in consegna ai propri figli: "dare loro le ali per volare rafforzando, allo stesso tempo, le loro radici".

Der Palazzo Frescobaldi, von dem aus man einen intimen Blick auf *Santo Spirito* werfen kann, atmet weiterhin den Geist des Geschlechts. Hier lebt das Erbe der Frescobaldis weiter und entwickelt sich stetig fort. Vom Palazzo aus wird auch das Weingeschäft betrieben. Die Geschäftsphilosophie der Frescobaldis zielt auf ein ständiges Modernisieren und genaues Analysieren von Methoden und traditionellen Denkstrukturen hin, um immer wieder Verbesserungen und Neuerungen in ihre Arbeit einfließen lassen zu können, ohne dabei die Kontinuität und die Verbindungen zu den vorhergehenden Generationen aus den Augen zu verlieren. „Wir laufen einen Marathon, und da ist es wichtiger, beständig weiterzulaufen und niemals stehen zu bleiben, als der Schnellste zu sein", erklärt Lamberto Frescobaldi. Die Familie sieht sich ihrer Geschichte verpflichtet und versteht ihre Schätze – eine wahrhaft reiche Vergangenheit, große Verantwortung und viele Privilegien – als einen Fundus, aus dem sie schöpft, anstatt ihn nur zu bewahren. Es soll ein Schatz sein, den sie später einmal ihren Kindern und Kindeskindern hinterlassen, damit diese ihrerseits das Beste daraus machen können. Sie möchten ihren Kindern „sowohl Flügel als auch Wurzeln" mitgeben, wie Eleonora Frescobaldi es schön formuliert.

Le palais Frescobaldi, qui bénéficie d'une vue privilégiée sur *Santo Spirito*, déborde de vie. L'héritage Frescobaldi continue à vivre ici, plus que jamais, et renforce l'histoire ininterrompue de la famille. Par ailleurs, la noble demeure est le siège de l'activité principale des Frescobaldi – le vin. Ces entrepreneurs ont pour philosophie de remettre à jour sans cesse leurs méthodes et leurs modes de pensée afin de les améliorer et de leur insuffler de nouvelles forces, tout en respectant le besoin de continuité avec les générations passées. Lamberto Frescobaldi déclare : « Nous sommes des coureurs de marathon et il est bien plus important de continuer sans s'arrêter que d'être le plus rapide ». Les Frescobaldi adhèrent à l'idée que ce dont ils bénéficient – leur riche histoire, leur responsabilité et leurs privilèges – est à eux pour être utilisé plutôt que possédé, afin d'être transmis, une fois leur temps passé, à leurs enfants et aux enfants de ceux-ci. Selon l'optique d'Eleonora Frescobaldi, il convient de donner à ses enfants « non seulement des racines, mais aussi des ailes ».

El palacio Frescobaldi, con su íntima y particular vista de la iglesia del *Santo Spirito*, es la residencia de la familia. El clan sigue viviendo allí y la tradición familiar perdura. El palacio acoge asimismo el negocio de los Frescobaldi: el vino. La filosofía de la familia aboga por el permanente cambio y el cuestionamiento de métodos y formas tradicionales de explotación para mejorar y fortalecer los negocios, al tiempo que respeta la continuidad con la labor de generaciones pasadas. Lamberto Frescobaldi opina: "Estamos corriendo una maratón y es más importante no pararse que ir deprisa". Los Frescobaldi adscriben la idea de que todo aquello que han recibido –el tesoro de su historia, la responsabilidad y los privilegios–, lo poseen únicamente en usufructo, y es su deber transmitirlo a sus hijos y a los hijos de sus hijos. Según Eleonora Frescobaldi, la mejor herencia para sus descendientes es "darles alas pero también raíces".

Eleonora and Lamberto Frescobaldi, *together with his mother, Bona, and sister, Diana, overlook the palace's courtyard.*

Eleonora e Lamberto Frescobaldi *osservano il cortile del palazzo insieme alla madre e alla sorella di lui, Bona e Diana.*

Eleonora und Lamberto Frescobaldi *blicken gemeinsam mit seiner Mutter Bona Frescobaldi und seiner Schwester Diana in den Innenhof des Palastes.*

Eleonora et Lamberto Frescobaldi *regardent la cour du palais avec la mère de Lamberto, Bona, et sa sœur Diana.*

Eleonora y Lamberto Frescobaldi *contemplan el patio del palacio en compañía de su madre, Bona, y su hermana, Diana.*

Castello di Nipozzano lies in the heart of the Chianti Rufina region and is a family business center. One of its striking features is the campanile of San Niccolò.

Il Castello di Nipozzano si trova nel cuore dell'area del Chianti Rufina, ed è il centro di gestione degli affari famigliari. Degno di nota il campanile di San Niccolò.

Castello di Nipozzano im Herzen der Region Chianti-Rufina ist ein Zentrum des Familienunternehmens. Zu den augenfälligsten Merkmalen gehört der Campanile von San Niccolò.

Le Castello di Nipozzano, qui se dresse au cœur de la région du Chianti Rufina, est un centre des activités commerciales de la famille – le campanile de San Niccolò en est l'un des traits les plus marquants.

El Castello de Nipozzano, situado en el corazón de la región de Chianti Rufina, es la sede de los negocios de la familia; uno de sus rasgos más distintivos es el campanario de San Niccolò.

Castello di Nipozzano, *Pelago*   53

Mansi

Villa Buonvisi / Villa Bernardini, Segromigno in Monte

The Mansi and Bernardini families' economic history is rich and varied, including coining for Italy's Emperors, investing in land, estates and agriculture and as merchants in the silk trade. The two families merged in the late 1800s when they were brought together by the marriage of the last heir to the Bernardini name, Antonietta, to the Marquis Raffaello Mansi. Their estate in the Lucchese Hills reflects generations of noble life, engaged in the family's many lucrative business ventures, artistic endeavors and entertaining. Their family's ancestor was one of many successful merchants that looked to the hills above the ancient, walled city of Lucca in the 1400s to create country estates, attracted to the country life while remaining near to Lucca, Pisa and the roads of commerce with Florence, Livorno and Rome. Villa Mansi, Villa Buonvisi and the Villa Bernardini in Segromigno in Monte are part of the larger historical estate of the Mansi Bernardini.

La storia delle fortune delle famiglie Mansi e Bernardini è ricca e variegata: furono coniatori per gli imperatori d'Italia, investirono denaro in terreni e proprietà, nel settore agricolo e, come mercanti, nel commercio della seta. Le due famiglie si unirono alla fine del XIX secolo grazie al matrimonio tra l'ultima erede dei Bernardini, Antonietta, e il marchese Raffaello Mansi. La loro tenuta sulle colline lucchesi ha visto crescere molte generazioni di nobili del casato, tutte assorbite dalla conduzione dei molti e remunerativi affari, ma anche amanti dell'arte e della mondanità. Il fondatore della famiglia fu uno dei tanti ricchi mercanti che nel XV secolo scelsero le colline che circondano l'antica città murata di Lucca per costruire la propria tenuta di campagna, attratto da una vita contadina che non fosse troppo lontana da città come la stessa Lucca o Pisa e, soprattutto, dalle tratte commerciali con Firenze, Livorno e Roma. Villa Mansi, Villa Buonvisi e Villa Bernardini a Segromigno in Monte sono solo una piccola parte dei possedimenti storici dei Mansi Bernardini.

In wirtschaftlicher Hinsicht kann die Geschichte der Familien Mansi und Bernardini als reich und vielgestaltig bezeichnet werden. Sie übernahmen die Münzprägung für die italienischen Herrscher, investierten in Boden, Güter und Landwirtschaft und waren als Kaufleute im Seidenhandel tätig. Die beiden Familien verbanden sich im späten 19. Jahrhundert, als die letzte Bernardini, Antonietta, den Marquis Raffaello Mansi heiratete. Ihr Landsitz in den Hügeln bei Lucca spiegelt nicht nur die Generationen von Patriziern wider, die dort einmal lebten, sondern auch ihren wirtschaftlichen Erfolg, ihre künstlerischen Bestrebungen und ihre Amüsements. Der Urvater der Familie gehörte zu jenen erfolgreichen Kaufmännern, die im 15. Jahrhundert die Hügel jenseits der Stadt Lucca mit ihrer antiken Stadtmauer als einen Ort ansahen, wo man Landgüter anlegen konnte. Dort vermochte man ein ländliches Leben zu führen und blieb doch in der Nähe von Lucca, Pisa und den Handelsrouten nach Florenz, Livorno und Rom. Die Villen Mansi, Buonvisi und Bernardini in Segromigno in Monte gehören alle zum großen Besitz der Mansi Bernardini.

Les Mansi et les Bernardini jouèrent un rôle majeur dans l'histoire économique de leur pays, puisqu'ils frappèrent monnaie pour les Empereurs, investirent dans la terre, l'immobilier et l'agriculture et pratiquèrent le commerce de la soie. Les deux familles fusionnèrent à la fin du XIXᵉ siècle, lorsque la dernière héritière des Bernardini, Antonietta, épousa le marquis Raffaello Mansi. Leur propriété située dans les collines de Lucques reflète des siècles de vie aristocratique, d'activités économiques lucratives, de passion pour les arts et de réceptions. Au XVᵉ siècle, l'ancêtre de la famille fut l'un de ces nombreux négociants qui eurent l'idée de quitter la cité de Lucques entourée de ses remparts pour s'installer à la campagne, dont le mode de vie les attirait, tout en restant près des routes commerciales reliant Florence, Livourne et Rome. Les villas Mansi, Buonvisi et Bernardini à Segromigno in Monte font partie des propriétés historiques des Mansi Bernardini.

La historia de la fortuna de los clanes Mansi y Bernardini es rica y variada; entre sus actividades se contaron la acuñación de moneda para los emperadores italianos, la inversión en tierras y haciendas en el sector agrícola, y el comercio de la seda. Las dos familias se unieron a finales del siglo XIX gracias al compromiso matrimonial entre la última heredera del clan Bernardini, Antonietta, y el marqués Raffaello Mansi. Su hacienda, emplazada en las colinas de Lucca, refleja generaciones de vida noble comprometidas con numerosas y lucrativas empresas comerciales, así como con actividades y entretenimientos artísticos. Uno de sus antepasados se contaba entre los exitosos comerciantes que se fijaron en las colinas de la antigua y amurallada ciudad de Lucca en el siglo XV como lugar idóneo para crear sus haciendas rústicas, en pleno campo pero no lejos de Lucca, Pisa y las rutas comerciales con Florencia, Livorno y Roma. Villa Mansi, Villa Buonvisi y Villa Bernardini, todas ellas cercanas a la localidad de Segromigno in Monte, son parte de la vasta e histórica hacienda de los Mansi Bernardini.

The entrance to Villa Buonvisi, one of the houses of the Mansi Bernardini estate. Details of the living room and the study.

Ingresso di Villa Buonvisi, una delle case della tenuta Mansi Bernardini. Particolari del salotto e dello studio.

Eingang zur Villa Buonvisi, eines der Gebäude auf dem Anwesen Mansi Bernardini. Detailansichten des Salons und des Arbeitszimmers.

L'entrée de la Villa Buonvisi, l'une des demeures des Mansi Bernardini. Détails de la salle de séjour et du cabinet de travail.

Recibidor de Villa Buonvisi, una de las casas pertenecientes a la estancia de Mansi Bernardini. Detalles de la sala y el estudio.

The façade of Villa Bernardini; the Bernardini coat of arms painted on a chair. A dressing table from a Villa Buonvisi bedroom.

Facciata di Villa Bernardini; stemma dei Bernardini dipinto su una sedia. Mobile toeletta in una delle camere da letto di Villa Buonvisi.

Die Fassade der Villa Bernardini; das Wappen der Bernardini auf einen Stuhl gemalt. Ein Toilettentisch in einem Schlafgemach der Villa Buonvisi.

La façade de la Villa Bernardini ; le blason des Bernardini peint sur un siège. Coiffeuse dans une chambre de la Villa Buonvisi.

Fachada de Villa Bernardini; escudo de armas de los Bernardini pintado en una silla. Tocador en un dormitorio de Villa Buonvisi.

The garden outside the limonaia (winter greenhouse) of Villa Bernardini is dominated by trees.

Alberi del giardino di Villa Bernardini nei pressi della limonaia, la serra invernale.

Im Garten vor der Limonaia (Wintergewächshaus) der Villa Bernardini ist durch den reichen Baumbestand geprägt.

Les arbres prédominent dans le jardin qui entoure la limonaia (serre hivernale) de la Villa Bernardini.

El jardín frente a la limonaia o invernáculo de Villa Bernardini está dominado por varios árboles.

Villa Mansi is currently undergoing careful restoration; the Villa dates to the 16th century, having undergone extensive restructuring in the mid 17th century. The Mansi family took ownership in 1675, and renovated the expansive gardens. In the beginning of the 1800s Villa Buonvisi became part of the estate as well. The Germans occupied Villa Bernardini and its neighboring villas during World War II (the 44th parallel crosses the mountain above), followed by the Americans during the winter of 1944/45. The American presence marked the time of a great and lasting romance between Laura Mansi and Leone Salom, an Italian naval officer. Having been discharged by the navy, Leone came through Tuscany and then traveled north to Venice (his hometown) with the Americans. But he made a lasting impression of Laura, and they eventually married and had seven children. In the present day, the Villas are the family homes for two branches of the modern Mansi Bernardini families. The care and upkeep of the estate also inspired the formation of Salogi, a villa vacation rental company.

Villa Mansi è attualmente in corso di restauro; l'edificio risale al XVI secolo ed è stato ampiamente ristrutturato alla metà del XVII secolo. La famiglia Mansi, che entrò in suo possesso nel 1675, ne ripristinò gli ampi giardini. All'inizio del XIX secolo anche Villa Buonvisi fu incorporata nella tenuta. Durante la Seconda Guerra Mondiale Villa Bernardini e gli edifici circostanti furono occupati prima dai tedeschi (la linea gotica passava proprio per la vicina montagna) e in seguito, nell'inverno tra il 1944 e il 1945, dagli americani. Fu in quest'ultimo periodo che nacque la grande storia d'amore tra Laura Mansi e Leone Salom, un ufficiale della marina italiana. Dopo il congedo dalla marina Leone attraversò la Toscana diretto a nord, verso la natale Venezia, al seguito dell'esercito americano. La sua permanenza lasciò però un ricordo indelebile nel cuore di Laura, e in seguito i due si sposarono ed ebbero sette figli. Oggi le ville sono abitate da due rami dell'attuale famiglia Mansi Bernardini. Dalla cura e dal mantenimento della tenuta è nata anche Salogi, un'agenzia attraverso la quale è possibile prenotare un soggiorno in questa e in altre ville della Toscana.

Die Villa Mansi wird augenblicklich sorgfältig restauriert. Sie stammt ursprünglich aus dem 16. Jahrhundert, wobei sie Mitte des 17. Jahrhunderts eingehend umgebaut wurde. Die Familie Mansi übernahm sie im Jahr 1675 und legte die großen Gärten neu an. Zu Beginn des 19. Jahrhunderts kam die Villa Buonvisi dazu. Im Zweiten Weltkrieg besetzten die deutschen Truppen die Villa Bernardini (der 44. Breitengrad verläuft über dem Berg oberhalb des Hauses), gefolgt von den Amerikanern im Winter 1944/45. Während dieser Zeit begann auch eine leidenschaftliche und dauerhafte Liebe zwischen Laura Mansi und Leone Salom, einem italienischen Marineoffizier. Leone Salom, der mit dem Ende des Krieges von der Marine ausgemustert worden war, kam in die Toskana und fuhr dann mit den Amerikanern weiter Richtung Norden nach Venedig (seine Heimatstadt). Er hinterließ einen derart starken Eindruck bei Laura Mansi, dass sie schließlich heirateten und sieben Kinder bekamen. Heute dienen die Villen als Wohnhäuser für zwei Linien der Mansi Bernardini. Die Verwaltung und Wartung des Landsitzes führte außerdem zur Entstehung von Salogi, einer Firma zur Vermittlung von Ferienvillen.

La villa Mansi, qui date du XVIe siècle et a été très remaniée au milieu du XVIIe, subit actuellement une restauration scrupuleuse. Les Mansi en firent l'acquisition en 1675 et firent redessiner l'immense parc. Ils devinrent propriétaires de la villa Buonvisi au début du XIXe siècle. Les Allemands occupèrent la Villa Bernardini pendant la Deuxième Guerre mondiale (le 44e parallèle traverse la colline qui la domine), suivis par les Américains pendant l'hiver 1944/1945. La présence américaine fut marquée par une grande et longue histoire d'amour entre Laura Mansi et Leone Salom, un officier de la marine italienne. Ayant été démobilisé, Leone traversa la Toscane puis se dirigea vers le Nord et Venise (sa ville natale) avec les Américains. Mais Laura ne devait pas l'oublier. Ils finirent par se marier et eurent sept enfants. Aujourd'hui, les deux branches actuelles de la famille Mansi Bernardini habitent dans les villas. Pour entretenir et préserver ce patrimoine, ils eurent l'idée de créer Salogi, une société de location de villas pour vacanciers.

En la actualidad se está restaurando cuidadosamente Villa Mansi, una casona que data del siglo XVI y que ya fue reestructurada a mediados del XVII. La familia Mansi la adquirió en 1675 y rediseñó sus extensos jardines. A comienzos del siglo XIX, Villa Buonvisi pasó asimismo a formar parte de la estancia. Los alemanes ocuparon Villa Bernardini y las fincas vecinas durante la Segunda Guerra Mundial (el paralelo 44 cruzaba la montañas cercanas), seguidos de los estadounidenses en el invierno de 1944/1945. La presencia norteamericana marcó el tiempo de un apasionado y duradero romance entre Laura Mansi y Leone Salom, un oficial de la marina italiana. Una vez licenciado del ejército, Leone cruzó tierras toscanas y viajó hacia el norte, a Venecia (su ciudad natal) con los estadounidenses. El joven causó una grata impresión a Laura. Ambos acabaron casándose y tuvieron siete hijos. En la actualidad, estas casonas acogen las residencias familiares de las dos ramas de la moderna familia Mansi Bernardini. El mantenimiento y cuidado de la hacienda inspiraron asimismo la creación de Salogi, una compañía especializada en el alquiler de alojamientos de lujo para las vacaciones.

Ricasoli

Castello di Brolio, Gaiole in Chianti

The iconic Brolio Castle draws thousands of visitors each year, some to see its Italianate gardens, others to stand in the history of one of Italy's greatest statesmen. Many know Brolio as the birthplace of modern Chianti Classico. Still more come to gaze at the castle's unique architectural progression through and melding of Medieval, Renaissance and Neo-Gothic styles, and its fortified walls attributed to Giuliano da Sangallo—powerful and archaic testaments to the centuries—long struggle for power among Florentine, Sienese and other neighboring fiefdoms. To the Ricasoli family, who has owned it for nine centuries, however, the castle is more than just a historical monument. In the mid 19th century, ancestor Bettino Ricasoli restructured the buildings, and moved his family to Brolio. And in a move that would resonant through generations, he began working with the wine. This "Thomas Jefferson of Italy" applied his love and talent for vines to substantially rejuvenate winemaking—and the area's hallmark wine—Chianti Classico—during his residence at Brolio.

Il Castello di Brolio attira ogni anno centinaia di turisti, che vengono ad ammirarne i giardini all'italiana o a visitare il luogo dove per tanti visse uno dei più grandi uomini politici d'Italia. Il Castello è famoso per aver dato i natali al moderno Chianti Classico, ma forse la maggior parte dei suoi visitatori è più interessata ad ammirarne incantata la commistione di stili architettonici (medievale, rinascimentale e neogotico) o le mura fortificate (antiche e imponenti testimonianze delle centenarie lotte di potere tra i fiorentini, i senesi e i feudi circostanti) progettate da Giuliano da Sangallo. Per la famiglia Ricasoli, proprietaria del castello per nove secoli, l'edificio è molto più di un semplice monumento storico. A metà del XIX secolo Bettino Ricasoli, uno degli avi del casato, restaurò il complesso e si trasferì a Brolio con la famiglia. Qui, con una decisione che avrebbe segnato il futuro dei Ricasoli, cominciò a lavorare il vino. Questo "Thomas Jefferson d'Italia", nel corso della sua permanenza al castello, sfruttò il suo amore e talento per la viticoltura per dare nuovo slancio alla produzione vinicola (e in particolare al Chianti Classico, prodotto simbolo della regione).

Das berühmte Schloss Brolio zieht jedes Jahr Tausende von Besucher an. Die einen kommen, um die italienischen Gärten zu bewundern, die anderen, um auf den Spuren eines der größten Staatsmänner Italiens zu wandeln. Aber noch mehr kommen, um die einzigartige architektonische Verbindung von Mittelalter, Renaissance und Neogotik oder die von Giuliano da Sangallo entworfenen Festungsmauern zu betrachten, die mächtige und archaisch anmutende Zeugnisse eines Jahrhunderte während Kampfs um die Macht zwischen Florentinern, Sienesen und benachbarten Fürstentümern darstellen. Viele kennen Brolio aber auch als die Geburtsstätte des modernen Chianti Classico. Für die Familie Ricasoli ist das Schloss allerdings mehr als ein bloßes historisches Monument; seit neun Jahrhunderten ist es in ihrem Besitz. Mitte des 19. Jahrhunderts ließ Bettino Ricasoli die Gebäude umbauen und bezog das Schloss mit seiner Familie. Mit diesem Umzug begann er auch mit der Weinkellerei, was sich auch durch die Generationen hinweg fortsetzen sollte. Dieser „italienische Thomas Jefferson" vermochte es mit seiner Begabung und seiner Liebe für den Wein dem gesamten Herstellungsprozess sowie dem berühmtesten Wein der Gegend – dem Chianti Classico – während seiner Jahre auf Brolio neues Leben einzuhauchen.

L'emblématique château de Brolio attire chaque année des milliers de visiteurs, certains désireux d'admirer son parc à l'italienne, les autres de marcher sur les pas de l'un des plus grands hommes d'État italiens. Pour beaucoup, Brolio est le berceau du chianti classico moderne. Ils sont encore plus nombreux à venir contempler l'exceptionnel cheminement architectural du château et son mélange de styles médiéval, Renaissance et néo-gothique, ainsi que ses enceintes élevées par Sangallo – témoignages puissants et archaïques des rivalités séculaires entre Florence, Sienne et leurs voisins. Cependant, pour la famille Ricasoli qui le possède depuis neuf siècles, le château est plus qu'un monument historique. Au milieu du XIXe siècle, Bettino Ricasoli fit remanier les bâtiments et installa sa famille à Brolio. Puis il se lança dans la viticulture, une activité qui devait marquer les générations à venir. Durant son séjour à Brolio, cet homme aux multiples talents appliqua son amour du vin et ses capacités à la rénovation de la viticulture, et en particulier du vin de la région, le chianti classico.

Miles de personas visitan cada año el emblemático castillo de Brolio, unas para admirar sus jardines italizantes, otras interesadas en la historia de uno de los más importantes políticos de Italia; hay quien conoce Brolio como el lugar de nacimiento del moderno Chianti Classico, pero los más acuden a contemplar la ecléctica arquitectura de estilos medievales, renacentistas y neogóticos, y las murallas fortificadas de Sangallo –poderoso y arcaico legado de las luchas por el poder acaecidas durante siglos entre Florencia, Siena y otros feudos vecinos. Sin embargo, el castillo es mucho más que un simple monumento histórico para la familia Ricasoli, que ha sido su propietaria durante novecientos años. A mediados del siglo XIX, un antepasado del clan, llamado Bettino Ricasoli, restructuró la construcción de los edificios y se mudó con su familia a Brolio. Y en una decisión que iba a tener consecuencias durante generaciones, empezó a producir vino. Mientras vivió en Brolio, este "Thomas Jefferson de Italia" puso todo su cariño y talento en la empresa de renovar substancialmente el negocio de la vitivinicultura y la denominación de origen del vino de la región –Chianti Classico.

Brolio Castle is surrounded by walls constructed in Renaissance times—too late for most of Brolio's contested history.

Il castello di Brolio è circondato da mura costruite in epoca rinascimentale, troppo tardi per gran parte della tormentata storia di Brolio.

Das Schloss Brolio ist von Mauern umgeben, die aus der Renaissance stammen und für einen Großteil der stürmischen Geschichte des Schlosses zu spät errichtet wurden.

Le château de Brolio est entouré d'enceintes construites à la Renaissance – trop tard pour l'histoire tumultueuse des Brolio.

El castillo de Brolio está rodeado por murallas construidas en tiempos del Renacimiento, demasiado tarde para la historia casi siempre llena de contiendas de los Brolio.

A painted armored figure and suited statue attest to Brolio's 500 years of battles. Other rooms illustrate the story of Brolio's coat of arms: the wallcovering of a rearing lion and horizontal red bands stem from the Ricasoli Meleto; the Ricasoli of Brolio added a stylized tower seen in the plaque.

Il guerriero dipinto in armatura e la statua accanto sono testimoni dei 500 anni di battaglie di Brolio. In altre stanze si ricostruisce la storia dello stemma di Brolio: l'arazzo con leone rampante e bande rosse trasversali risale alla famiglia Ricasoli Meleto, mentre i Ricasoli di Brolio aggiunsero allo scudo una torre stilizzata.

Ein gemalter Ritter und eine Statue in Rüstung spielen auf 500 Jahre kriegerischer Auseinandersetzungen um Brolio an. In anderen Räumen kann man der Geschichte des Familienwappens verfolgen: Die Tapeten mit einem brüllenden Löwen und horizontalen roten Bändern stammen von der Familie Ricasoli Meleto, während die Ricasoli von Brolio einen stilisierten Turm, wie auf dem Schild, hinzufügten.

Ce tableau et cette statue de guerriers en armure témoignent des 500 ans de vie militaire chez les Brolio. Les autres pièces illustrent l'histoire des armoiries des Brolio : le revêtement mural figurant un lion dressé et des bandes rouges horizontales date de la famille Ricasoli Meleto ; les Ricasoli de Brolio ajoutèrent la tour stylisée visible sur la plaque.

Una estatua pintada y vestida con una armadura da fe de los 500 años de batallas de los Brolio. Otras salas ilustran la historia del escado de armas del clan: el león erguido y las bandas rojas horizontales del tapiz se remontan a los tiempos de la familia Ricasoli Meleto; los Ricasoli de Brolio añadieron una estilizada torre que se aprecia en la placa.

Francesco Ricasoli took the helm of Brolio's winemaking in 1993. Francesco, formerly a successful commercial photographer, came to this vast undertaking—as Bettino, the "Iron Baron" had a century and a half before—with no direct experience in the wine business. Reclaiming and reenergizing Brolio's innovative winemaking tradition is a great challenge. Like the castle, the wine must be enduring while living in its own time, and exude a character that exemplifies the stature of its heritage and place. Francesco is transforming the wines, from restructuring the cellars from a giant storehouse to a modern art piece to restoring the vineyards and reinvigorating the taste and life of the wine.

Francesco Ricasoli ha preso le redini dell'azienda di famiglia nel 1993. Dopo aver lavorato con successo come fotografo, si è dedicato a questa impresa titanica senza avere alcuna esperienza diretta del mestiere (proprio come aveva fatto Bettino, detto "il barone di ferro", un secolo e mezzo prima di lui). Riappropriarsi dell'innovativa tradizione di Brolio e infonderle nuova vita non era impresa facile. Proprio come il castello, il vino deve resistere nel tempo pur rimanendo ancorato al presente; e deve possedere un carattere che ne metta in risalto la nobiltà e la grande tradizione. Francesco ha rinfoltito le vigne, trasformato le cantine da gigantesco magazzino a moderno capolavoro artistico e rinnovato il gusto e il vigore delle uve.

1993 übernahm Francesco Ricasoli die Führung im Familienunternehmen. Der erfolgreiche Fotograf stieg ebenso wie sein Vorfahre Bettino Ricasoli – der „Eiserne Baron" anderthalb Jahrhunderte vor ihm – ohne wirkliches Vorwissen und Erfahrung ins Weingeschäft ein. Sich auf Brolios innovative Tradition in der Weinherstellung zu besinnen und ihr neuen Aufschwung zu geben, stellt eine große Herausforderung dar. Wie das Schloss muss auch der Wein Bestand haben, ohne dabei das Heute zu vergessen; er muss seine Persönlichkeit beweisen, welche sein Erbe und seinen Herkunftsort widerspiegelt. Francesco Ricasoli verändert die Weine, indem er aus den gewaltigen Lagerräumen im Keller ein modernes Kunstwerk macht, die Weinberge umstrukturiert und dem Wein neuen Geschmack und neues Leben verleiht.

Francesco Ricasoli prit la tête du vignoble de Brolio en 1993. Après une carrière brillante dans la photographie commerciale, Francesco se lança dans cette vaste entreprise tout comme Bettino, le « baron de fer », 150 ans plus tôt – c'est-à-dire sans expérience directe de la viticulture. Insuffler une nouvelle vigueur à la tradition vinicole innovante de Brolio constitue un défi majeur. Tout comme le château, le vin doit durer tout en étant de son époque et révéler un caractère à la hauteur de la stature de son héritage et de son terroir. Francesco fait évoluer les vins, restructure les caves – un entrepôt géant dont il a fait une œuvre d'art moderne –, restaure les vignes et redonne du goût et de la vie à son vin.

Francesco Ricasoli tomó el relevo de la explotación vinícola de Brolio en 1993. Francesco, que era un exitoso fotógrafo publicitario, decidió iniciar esta vasta empresa tal y como lo había hecho un siglo y medio antes su antepasado Bettino, el "Barón de hierro": sin experiencia ninguna en el negocio del vino. Retomar y revitalizar la innovadora tradición vinícola de Brolio es un gran reto. Como el castillo, el vino debe perdurar sin dejar por ello de vivir en su tiempo y presentar un carácter que ejemplifique la estatura de su linaje y terruño. Francesco está transformando las formas de producción, desde la reestructuración de la bodega, que ya no es simplemente un enorme almacén sino una moderna obra de arte, hasta la recuperación de cepas, todo ello para darle al vino más vida y sabor.

Antinori

Palazzo Antinori, Firenze

Recorded as early as 1188 living in the small town of Calenzano, the Antinori family moved to Florence in the early 13th century. In 1385, Giovanni di Piero Antinori made official what would be his family's centuries-long obsession—wine making—by registering with the Florentine vintners' guild. In the mid 1900s Niccolò Antinori (and his brother in law, Mario Incisa della Rocchetta) experimented with the idea of introducing French varietal grapes into Tuscany with the goal of producing fine wines with Italian character. When Niccolò's son, Piero, took over the family business in the 1960s, he began to introduce French wine making techniques as well. The Antinori family's innovative thinking has reaped rewards, both for the Antinori wine tradition, as well as for the world of wine lovers. The wine company and its many estates are managed from Palazzo Antinori, which functions as the business and family center. It was built around 1470 and came into the Antinori family in 1506.

La famiglia Antinori, che le cronache collocano nella cittadina di Calenzano sin dal 1188, si spostò a Firenze agli inizi del XIII secolo. Nel 1385 Giovanni di Piero Antinori, unendosi alla corporazione dei vinai fiorentini, rese ufficiale quell'ossessione per il vino che sarebbe diventata l'amore esclusivo della sua famiglia nei secoli a venire. A metà del XX secolo Niccolò Antinori (insieme al cognato Mario Incisa della Rocchetta), deciso a esplorare nuove strade, introdusse in Toscana le uve francesi, con l'intento di produrre vini pregiati dal carattere tipicamente italiano. Quando Piero, figlio di Niccolò, ereditò l'azienda di famiglia negli anni 1960, importò dai francesi anche le tecniche di produzione. Le idee innovative della famiglia Antinori hanno ottenuto grandi riconoscimenti che hanno premiato la tradizione vinicola del casato e fatto la gioia degli amanti del vino di tutto il mondo. L'azienda di famiglia e le sue numerose succursali vengono gestite direttamente da Palazzo Antinori, che funge dunque sia da ufficio che da abitazione. Il palazzo risale al 1470 circa ed è diventato proprietà degli Antinori nel 1506.

Erstmals wurde die Familie Antinori 1188 urkundlich erwähnt, als ihre Vorfahren in der kleinen Stadt Calenzano lebten. Sie übersiedelten aber bereits im frühen 13. Jahrhundert nach Florenz. Im Jahr 1385 meldete sich Giovanni di Piero Antinori offiziell bei der Florentiner Weinzunft als Winzer an. Die Weinherstellung sollte auch in den darauffolgenden Jahrhunderten die Leidenschaft dieser Familie bleiben. Mitte des 20. Jahrhunderts versuchte Niccolò Antinori (und sein Schwager Mario Incisa della Rocchetta) zum ersten Mal, französische Rebsorten in der Toskana anzusiedeln, um hochwertige Weine mit italienischem Charakter zu produzieren. Als Niccolòs Sohn Piero in den 1960er-Jahren das Familienunternehmen übernahm, führte er bestimmte französische Techniken der Weinherstellung ein. Dieses innovative Handeln der Familie Antinori hat nicht nur Früchte für sie selber und ihre Weintradition getragen, sondern auch für die Weinliebhaber in der ganzen Welt. Das Unternehmen mit seinen zahlreichen Weingütern wird vom Palazzo Antinori aus verwaltet, der als Geschäfts- und als Familiensitz dient. Er wurde um 1470 erbaut und von den Antinoris im Jahr 1506 erworben.

La famille Antinori, qui est documentée dès 1188 dans la petite ville de Calenzano, partit vivre à Florence au début du XIIIe siècle. En 1385, Giovanni di Piero Antinori rendit officiel ce qui devait se révéler l'obsession séculaire de sa famille – la viticulture – en devenant membre de la corporation des vignerons de Florence. Au milieu de XXe siècle, Niccolò Antinori (et son beau-frère, Mario Incisa della Rocchetta) furent tentés par une expérimentation et introduisirent des cépages français en Toscane, en vue d'obtenir des vins fins dotés d'un caractère italien. Lorsque Piero, le fils de Niccolò, prit la tête de l'entreprise familiale dans les années 1960, il décida d'introduire aussi des techniques viticoles françaises. L'audace des Antinori a porté ses fruits, tant pour la tradition viticole Antinori que pour les amateurs de leurs produits. L'entreprise viticole et ses nombreux domaines sont gérés depuis le palais Antinori, qui tient lieu de siège commercial et de foyer familial. Construit vers 1470, il appartient aux Antinori depuis 1506.

Las primeras noticias del clan de los Antinori se remontan nada más y nada menos que al año 1188, cuando vivían en la pequeña localidad de Calenzano, desde la que se mudaron a Florencia a comienzos del siglo XIII. En 1385, Giovanni di Piero Antinori dio carácter oficial a la que sería una pasión familiar centenaria –la elaboración de vinos– al registrarse en el gremio de vinateros florentinos. Hacia mediados del siglo XX, Niccolò Antinori (y su cuñado, Mario Incisa della Rocchetta) introdujeron variedades de uva francesas para intentar lograr caldos finos con carácter italiano. Cuando el hijo de Niccolò, Piero, se hizo cargo de los negocios familiares en la década de 1960, adoptó asimismo técnicas vitivinícolas francesas. La filosofía innovadora de los Antinori ha cosechado premios tanto para la tradición vinícola familiar como para el mundo de los amantes del vino en general. La compañía vitivinícola y sus numerosas estancias están dirigidas desde el Palazzo Antinori, sede del negocio y centro de la vida familiar. El palacio fue construido hacia 1470 y es propiedad del clan desde 1506.

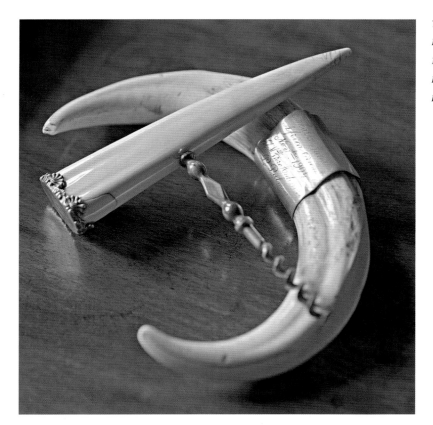

The study of Niccolò Antinori: *his desk is as he left it before he died.*

Lo studio di Niccolò Antinori, *con la scrivania lasciata com'era prima della morte.*

Niccolò Antinoris *Arbeitszimmer. Sein Schreibtisch blieb seit seinem Tod unverändert.*

Le cabinet de travail *de Niccolò Antinori : son bureau est tel qu'il l'a laissé à sa mort.*

Estudio de Niccolò Antinori: *su escritorio está tal y como lo dejó antes de morir.*

Sitting room on the third floor of Palazzo Antinori, the family seat with offices and living quarters since 1506. The tapestries are copriporte (door covers), dating from the 1600s, which formerly belonged to the Riccardi family.

Salotto al terzo piano di Palazzo Antinori, abitazione e ufficio della famiglia sin dal 1506. Gli arazzi sono copriporte del XVII secolo provenienti dalla famiglia Riccardi.

Salon im dritten Stock des Palazzo Antinori, in dem die Familie seit 1506 lebt und ihre Geschäfte verwaltet. Bei den Wandteppichen handelt es sich um sogenannte Copriporte (Türbehänge), die aus dem 17. Jahrhundert von der Familie Riccardi stammen.

Salon au troisième étage du Palazzo Antinori, qui abrite les bureaux et la résidence de la famille depuis 1506. Les tapisseries ou copriporte (portières) proviennent de la famille Riccardi et datent du XVIIe siècle.

Salón en el tercer piso del palacio Antinori, sede y residencia familiar desde 1506. Los tapices copriporte (cubre-puertas) datan de! siglo XVII y provienen de la familia Riccardi.

The portrait on wood above the mantel is by a Flemish master of the 16th century. Allegra Antinori riding on the beach on the Maremma coast between Bolgheri and Castagneto Carducci, near the Guado al Tasso estate.

Il ritratto su tavola sopra al camino è opera di pittore fiammingo del XVI secolo. Allegra Antinori a cavallo sulla spiaggia della costa maremmana fra Bolgheri e Castagneto Carducci, nei pressi della tenuta di Guado al Tasso.

Das Porträt auf Holz, das über dem Kamin hängt, stammt von einem flämischen Meister aus dem 16. Jahrhundert. Allegra Antinori reitet den Strand zwischen Bolgheri und Castagneto Carducci an der Maremma-Küste entlang, ganz in der Nähe des Landsitzes Guado al Tasso.

Au-dessus du manteau de la cheminée, ce portrait peint sur un panneau de bois est dû à un maître flamand du XVIe siècle. Allegra Antinori chevauchant sur une plage de la côte de la Maremme, entre Bolgheri et Castagneto Carducci, à proximité de la propriété de Guado al Tasso.

El retrato en madera sobre la repisa de la chimenea es de un maestro flamenco del siglo XVI. Allegra Antinori cabalgando en una playa de la costa de Maremma entre Bolgheri y Castagneto Carducci, cerca de la hacienda Guado al Tasso.

Currently, Marchese Piero Antinori's three daughters, Albiera, Allegra, and Alessia, represent the 26th generation to participate in the Antinori family business. A bedrock of family, honoring every generation's contribution, combined with an indelible imprint of the land has kept the lineage going. Each generation has successfully passed along its love of the land to succeeding generations; in the Antinori family, this means an understanding and appreciation for nature and its rhythms, and a devotion to the Italian countryside steeped in the pleasures and agonies of agriculture. Allegra notes one additional motivation: "There is responsibility, too, for the family, for those who have come before, as well as to those who will follow you."

Attualmente le tre figlie del marchese Piero Antinori, Albiera, Allegra e Alessia, rappresentano la ventiseiesima generazione di viticoltori della famiglia. Il loro legame con il passato è solido e indissolubile e ha permesso alla famiglia di mantenere vive le proprie trazioni, grazie alle conoscenze acquisite nei secoli e al legame profondo con il territorio. Gli antenati del casato sono infatti riusciti a trasmettere ai loro successori l'amore per una terra fonte di grandi soddisfazioni ma anche di grandi sacrifici, una passione che significa comprensione e rispetto della natura e dei suoi ritmi. Allegra aggiunge anche che questo amore significa "senso di responsabilità, verso la famiglia, verso chi ci ha preceduto e chi verrà dopo di noi".

Heutzutage repräsentieren die drei Töchter des Marchese Piero Antinori – Albiera, Allegra und Alessia – die 26. Generation, die im Familienunternehmen mitwirkt. Es herrscht eine enge Familienbande, die durch die vorangegangenen Generationen ebenso geprägt wird wie durch das umgebende Land. Die Liebe für das Land wurde von einer Generation an die nächste weitergegeben, und bedeutet für die Familie Antinori eine hohe Wertschätzung für die Natur und ihre Jahreszeiten sowie Demut gegenüber der italienischen Landschaft, die ihnen durch die Landwirtschaft nicht nur Freude, sondern auch Leid gebracht hat. „Außerdem verspüren wir alle Verantwortung für die Familie – für jene, die vor uns kamen und für jene, die uns nachfolgen werden", fügt Allegra als weitere Motivation hinzu.

Aujourd'hui, les trois filles du marquis Piero Antinori, Albiera, Allegra et Alessia, représentent la 26e génération à participer à l'entreprise familiale. La solidité de la famille, qui rend hommage à la contribution de chaque génération, associée à la marque indélébile du terroir, a perpétué la lignée. Chaque génération a réussi à transmettre à la suivante son amour du pays ; chez les Antinori, cela signifie comprendre et apprécier la nature et ses rythmes, mais aussi aimer la campagne italienne avec ses plaisirs et les affres de l'agriculture. Allegra signale une autre motivation : « Nous avons par ailleurs une responsabilité envers la famille, envers ceux qui nous ont précédé, de même qu'envers ceux qui nous suivront ».

En la actualidad las tres hijas del marqués Piero Antinori —Albiera, Allegra y Alessia—, representan la vigésimo sexta generación encargada de los negocios del clan. Un fuerte fundamento familiar que honra la contribución de cada generación, combinado con la indeleble impronta de la tierra, ha permitido la perpetuación del linaje y su herencia. Cada generación ha logrado transmitir el amor por la tierra a las siguientes. En la familia Antinori, eso se traduce en el entendimiento y aprecio de la naturaleza y sus ritmos vitales, así como en una gran devoción por el campo italiano dividido entre el placer y la agonía de la agricultura. Allegra indica una motivación suplementaria: "Tenemos también una responsabilidad para con la familia, para con todos los que nos han precedido y los que nos sucederán".

Serristori

Villa Olmaia, San Vincenzo

The Serristori family has leant political and military leadership as well as literary scholarship in its centuries of history in Tuscany. During the Renaissance, Averardo di Antonio Serristori (1497–1569) served in diplomatic posts, notably Ambassador for Cosimo I de' Medici to Rome. Another storied family member, Count Luigi Serristori (1793–1857) was a major figure in the *Risorgimento*, the 19th century Italian unification movement. He was a prolific author of books and articles on many topics, including travel, economics, statistics, and the first Italian work on steam engines and steamships. In more recent years, Averardo Serristori enjoys a peaceful retreat at Villa Olmaia near the Tuscan coast.

Sono molti i membri della famiglia Serristori che hanno influenzato la storia politica e militare della Toscana, oltre che la sua letteratura. Durante il rinascimento Averardo di Antonio Serristori (1497–1569) ricoprì molti incarichi diplomatici, e in particolare quello di ambasciatore di Cosimo I de' Medici a Roma. Un'altro storico membro della famiglia, il conte Luigi Serristori (1793–1857), fu invece una delle grandi figure del risorgimento. Scrisse numerosi libri e articoli sugli argomenti più disparati, dai viaggi all'economia, dalla statistica al primo trattato italiano sui motori e le navi a vapore. In tempi più recenti, l'attuale Averardo Serristori vive in piacevole ritiro a Villa Olmaia, sulla costa toscana.

Die Familie Serristori hat über die Jahrhunderte hinweg großen Einfluss auf die politischen und militärischen Geschicke der Toskana ausgeübt und auch bedeutsame literarische Beiträge geliefert. Während der Renaissance diente Averardo di Antonio Serristori (1497–1569) als Diplomat, vor allem jedoch als Botschafter Cosimo I. de' Medici in Rom. Ein weiteres berühmtes Familienmitglied, Graf Luigi Serristori (1793–1857), spielte eine bedeutsame Rolle im *Risorgimento*, der italienischen Vereinigungsbewegung im 19. Jahrhundert. Er war zudem ein überaus produktiver Schriftsteller, der Bücher und Aufsätze zu vielen Themen wie zum Beispiel über Reisen, Ökonomie und Statistik sowie das erste italienische Werk über Dampfmaschinen und Dampfschiffe verfasste. Heutzutage genießt Averardo Serristori die Rückzugsmöglichkeiten, die ihm die Villa Olmaia in der Nähe der toskanischen Küste bietet.

Tout au long de l'histoire de la Toscane, les Serristori se sont distingués par leur valeur militaire et politique, ainsi que par leur érudition. À la Renaissance, Averardo di Antonio Serristori (1497–1569) fit carrière dans la diplomatie et fut entre autre ambassadeur de Côme I de Médicis à Rome. Le comte Luigi Serristori (1793–1857), autre membre illustre de la famille, joua un rôle de premier plan pendant le *Risorgimento*, le mouvement d'unification italienne au XIXe siècle. Il fut un auteur prolifique de livres et d'articles sur les sujets les plus divers, voyages, économie, statistiques et on lui doit le premier ouvrage italien sur les machines et les bateaux à vapeur. Depuis quelques années, Averardo Serristori jouit d'une retraite bien méritée à la Villa Olmaia, près de la côte toscane.

La familia Serristori ha abanderado durante siglos el poder político y militar, así como la erudición literaria en la Toscana. Durante el Renacimiento, Averardo di Antonio Serristori (1497–1569) ocupó diversos puestos diplomáticos, entre ellos el de embajador de Cosme I de Médicis en Roma. Otro famoso miembro del linaje, el conde Luigi Serristori (1793–1857), fue una importante figura del *Risorgimento* o movimiento de unificación de Italia iniciado en el siglo XIX. Este personaje fue asimismo un prolífico autor de libros y artículos sobre los más diversos temas, por ejemplo, viajes, economía y estadística, y del primer tratado italiano sobre motores y barcos de vapor. En nuestros días, Averardo Serristori disfruta de un apacible retiro en Villa Olmaia, junto a la costa toscana.

A simply decorated bedroom with a painting of Averardo Serristori's father, Giancarlo. Artwork abounds in the villa, Averardo's Rhodesian ridgeback being the subject of one painting.

Una camera da letto dall'arredo semplice, con un quadro del padre di Averardo Serristori, Giancarlo. Numerose sono le opere d'arte esposte nella villa; un dipinto ha come soggetto il Rhodesian Ridgeback di Averardo.

Ein schlichtes Schlafzimmer mit einem Porträt von Averardo Serristoris Vater Giancarlo. Überall in der Villa finden sich Kunstwerke; auf einem Bild ist der Rhodesian Ridgeback des Hausherrn verewigt.

Une chambre décorée avec simplicité, ornée d'un portrait de Giancarlo, père d'Averardo Serristori. La villa regorge d'œuvres d'art ; l'un des tableaux représente un chien de chasse de Rhodésie, favori d'Averardo.

Una alcoba de decoración sencilla con el retrato del padre de Averardo Serristori, Giancarlo. Las obras de arte abundan en la villa; el perro de Averardo, un Ridgeback de Rodesia, es el tema de uno de los cuadros.

Villa Olmaia pays homage both to modern art and the days of big-game hunting: the painting "Love" hangs in the shadow of a record African water buffalo trophy.

Villa Olmaia testimonia dell'amore per l'arte moderna e la caccia: il dipinto "Amore" è appeso sotto il trofeo di un imponente bufalo africano.

Die Villa Olmaia ist ganz der modernen Kunst und den Tagen der Großwildjagd gewidmet. Das Bild „Liebe" hängt im Schatten einer gewaltigen Trophäe eines afrikanischen Wasserbüffels.

La Villa Olmaia rend hommage à l'art moderne et à l'époque des grands safaris — un tableau intitulé « L'amour » côtoie une dépouille exceptionnelle de buffle d'eau africain.

Villa Olmaia presta homenaje al arte moderno y a los tiempos de la caza mayor. La pintura "Amor" cuelga a la sombra del trofeo de un búfalo de agua recuerdo de África.

Serristori and his Traxler ancestors, including his grandmother depicted on her wedding day, his grandfather Augusto Traxler and Manfredi Traxler in green frame.

Serristori e i suoi antenati Traxler, fra cui la nonna nel giorno del suo matrimonio, il nonno Augusto Traxler e Manfredi Traxler nella cornice verde.

Serristori und seine Vorfahren aus der Familie Traxler – einschließlich seiner Großmutter an ihrem Hochzeitstag, seinem Großvater Augusto Traxler und Manfredi Traxler im grünen Rahmen.

Serristori et ses ancêtres Traxler – notamment sa grand-mère le jour de son mariage, son grand-père Augusto Traxler et Manfredi Traxler dans un cadre vert.

Serristori y varios de los antepasados Traxler, entre ellos la abuela el día de su boda, al abuelo Augusto Traxler y Manfredi Traxler en verde.

A view into the private courtyard where Serristori plays with the German shepherd Lulu, one of the estate's many dogs.

Vista del cortile privato; Serristori con il pastore tedesco Lulu, uno dei molti cani che vivono alla villa.

Ein Blick auf den Innenhof, wo Serristori mit dem Schäferhund Lulu, einem der vielen Hunde des Anwesens, spielt.

Vue sur la cour privée où Serristori joue avec un berger allemand, Lulu, l'un des nombreux chiens de la propriété.

Una vista del patio particular donde Serristori juega con un pastor alemán llamado Lulu, uno de los muchos perros de la estancia.

In its Maremma seaside country setting replete with Tuscan villas, Serristori's atypical 20th century villa reflects the passions of his parents. Villa Olmaia is reminiscent of the colonial bungalows of East Africa, with long, low rooflines, and a large shaded veranda overlooking the lawn, and its floors of teak, taken from the deck of an Italian warship. Its sprawling footprint is set around an interior courtyard whose walls are stone blocks hewn from the family's quarry. Many features exude and celebrate the life of the big game hunt, beyond the style of the home. Hunt trophies celebrating the passion of Averardo's late father Giancarlo, abound: massive, 150-pound elephant tusks create an arched entry to greet visitors in the foyer, and his hunting gear occupies the tack room. Even Giancarlo's wife, Ginevra's love of dogs seems to hearken back; stately Irish Wolfhounds, a traditional war and hunting dog (though they are not used for this purpose today) predominate, bounding happily in the villa's lawn.

L'atipica tenuta dei Serristori, costruita nel XX secolo, si trova sulla costa maremmana, circondata da numerose altre ville. L'edificio rispecchia le grandi passioni dei suoi creatori. Villa Olmaia ricorda i bungalow coloniali dell'Africa orientale, con i suoi tetti lunghi e bassi, le grandi e ombreggiate verande che guardano il prato e i suoi pavimenti in teak, realizzati con le assi del ponte di una nave da guerra italiana. La sua pianta irregolare si sviluppa attorno a un cortile interno cinto da mura, realizzate con macigni intagliati nella cava di famiglia. Sono molti i particolari della casa, architettura a parte, a ricordare le grandi battute di caccia. Le sue sale sono infatti ricolme dei trofei che celebrano la grande passione per la caccia di Giancarlo, il defunto padre di Averardo: le gigantesche zanne di elefante (pesanti 70 chili) che formano l'arco d'entrata che accoglie i visitatori nel foyer, oppure il suo equipaggiamento da cacciatore conservato nella stanza dei cimeli. La villa non ha dimenticato però neanche il grande amore di Ginevra, moglie di Giancarlo: gli imponenti levrieri irlandesi, razza storicamente addestrata al combattimento e alla caccia dei lupi (anche se oggi non più), e che ancor oggi continuano a correre vivaci sul prato della casa.

Am Küstenlandstrich der Maremma, wo viele toskanische Landhäuser zu finden sind, steht auch Averardo Serristoris recht untypische Villa aus dem 20. Jahrhundert, die nach dem Geschmack seiner Eltern errichtet wurde. Mit ihren langgezogenen, flachen Dächern, der großen Veranda, die sich zu einem gepflegten Rasen öffnet, und dem Teakholzboden, der vom Deck eines italienischen Kriegsschiffs stammt, erinnert die Villa an die eingeschossigen kolonialen Häuser Ostafrikas. Das große Haus ist um einen Innenhof herum angelegt, dessen Mauern aus Steinblöcken erbaut wurden, die aus dem Steinbruch der Familie stammen. Viele Details weisen auf eine Passion für die Großwildjagd in Afrika hin. So spiegelt die große Sammlung an Jagdtrophäen die Jagdleidenschaft von Averardo Serristoris verstorbenem Vater Giancarlo wider: Gewaltige, 70 Kilo schwere Elefantenstoßzähne begrüßen als Eingangstor im Foyer den Besucher und die Jagdausrüstung ziert die Geschirrkammer des Pferdestalls. Auch die Liebe von Giancarlo Serristoris Ehefrau Ginevra zu Hunden prägt noch heute das Bild der Villa. Herrschaftliche irische Wolfshunde – traditionelle Kampf- und Jagdhunde, die jedoch nicht mehr zu diesen Zwecken gehalten werden – tollen fröhlich über den Rasen.

Sur ce littoral de la Maremme si riche en villas toscanes, cette demeure atypique du XXe siècle reflète les passions de ses parents. La Villa Olmaia évoque les bungalows coloniaux d'Afrique de l'Est avec ses toitures longues et basses et sa vaste véranda ombragée qui donne sur la pelouse, ou ses planchers en teck, prélevés sur le pont d'un navire de guerre italien. Sa surface généreuse s'organise autour d'une cour intérieure dont les murs sont constitués de blocs de pierre provenant de la carrière familiale. Outre le style de la demeure, de nombreux détails révèlent et célèbrent la chasse au gros gibier. Les nombreux trophées rappellent l'amour pour la chasse de feu le père d'Averardo, Giancarlo : d'énormes défenses d'éléphant pesant 70 kilos créent une arche qui accueille les visiteurs dans l'entrée, tandis que son équipement de chasse accapare la sellerie. Même l'amour pour les chiens de Ginevra, l'épouse de Giancarlo, semble perpétuer ce goût ; ses magnifiques lévriers irlandais, chiens traditionnels de guerre et de chasse (bien qu'ils soient élevés dans des intentions plus pacifiques aujourd'hui) règnent en maîtres sur les pelouses de la villa.

En esta zona del litoral de Maremma salpicada de villas toscanas, la atípica casona de Serristori, levantada en el siglo XX, refleja la pasión de sus antecesores. Villa Olmaia es una reminiscencia de los *bungalows* coloniales del África oriental con su tejado de líneas planas y anchas, la amplia veranda umbría orientada al césped del jardín y el suelo de teca extraída de un antiguo buque de guerra italiano. La planta del edificio se extiende alrededor de un patio interior, cuyos muros están formados por bloques de piedra extraídos de la cantera familiar. Como colofón al estilo de la casa, ciertos elementos reflejan y celebran el deporte de la caza mayor. Abundan los trofeos que dan fe de la pasión del difunto padre de Averardo, Giancarlo: unos colmillos de elefante macizos de unos 70 kilos forman un arco que da la bienvenida a las visitas en el recibidor y su equipo de caza ocupa el cuarto de los aperos del establo. Incluso el amor por los perros de Ginevra, la esposa de Giancarlo, parece estar en consonancia con el entorno; sus majestuosos lobos irlandeses (una raza tradicionalmente muy apreciada para la caza, así como en los conflictos bélicos, aunque hoy en día ya no se utiliza con ese fin), llaman la atención correteando alegres por el césped de la villa.

Torrigiani

Palazzo Torrigiani del Campuccio, Firenze

The Palazzo or Casino Torrigiani del Campuccio is known not just by the tower on its adorning coat of arms, but also by the fanciful tower that peeks over its garden walls. The inspiring garden was designed and built by a succession of talented architects, including Luigi Cambray d'Igny, Gaetano Baccani, and Bernardo Fallani in the early 19th century. It is the largest privately owned walled garden inside any city in Europe and conceals other secrets and treasures. The remains of Florence's bastions from the time of Cosimo I (which formerly reached Fort Belvedere) hide under decades of vines, while sculptures and pathways beckon to family friends, artists and garden aficionados. The *rondo* of the garden is built around a statue of Pietro Torrigiani and his son Luigi, and is oriented precisely to the four directions, with individual statues representing each season.

Il Palazzo Torrigiani del Campuccio, noto anche come Casino Torrigiani, non deve la sua fama esclusivamente alla torre che campeggia sullo stemma di famiglia, ma anche alla stravagante torre che spunta dalla cinta muraria del suo parco. Il suggestivo giardino fu concepito e realizzato ai primi del XIX secolo da diversi architetti di grande talento, tra i quali Luigi Cambray d'Igny, Gaetano Baccani e Bernardo Fallani. Si tratta del più grande giardino circondato da mura che si trovi in una città europea e vanta molti segreti e tesori nascosti. Tra questi i resti dei bastioni delle mura di Firenze, risalenti all'epoca di Cosimo I (e che arrivavano fino a Forte Belvedere), da decenni ormai celati alla vista sotto i rampicanti. Le sue sculture e i suoi sentieri continuano ad attirare amici di famiglia, artisti e amanti dei bei giardini. I vialetti del rondò quadripartito del parco, con al centro la statua di Pietro Torrigiani e del figlio Luigi, sono orientati in direzione dei quattro punti cardinali e sono segnalati ciascuno da una statua che rappresenta una delle quattro stagioni.

Der Palazzo bzw. das Casino Torrigiani del Campuccio ist bekannt für den Turm, der das Wappen schmückt, aber auch für den phantasievollen Turm, der über seine Gartenmauern weit hinausragt. Dieser schöne Garten wurde von mehreren begabten Architekten entworfen und angelegt. Dazu gehörten im frühen 19. Jahrhundert u. a. Luigi Cambray d'Igny, Gaetano Baccani und Bernardo Fallani. Es ist Europas größter, von Mauern umgebener, städtischer Privatgarten, und er verbirgt so manches Geheimnis und so manchen Schatz. Die Überreste der florentinischen Stadtmauern aus der Zeit Cosimo I. (die ursprünglich bis zum Forte di Belvedere reichten) verstecken sich unter seit Jahrzehnten wuchernden Kletterpflanzen, während Skulpturen und überwachsene Pfade Freunde der Familie, Künstler und Gartenliebhaber zum Verweilen einladen. Den Mittelpunkt des Gartens bildet ein Rondell mit einem Standbild Pietro Torrigianis und seines Sohnes Luigi. Von diesem gehen Achsen in alle Himmelsrichtungen ab, die auf Skulpturen der vier Jahreszeiten zulaufen.

Le Palazzo ou Casino Torrigiani del Campuccio est connu non seulement par la tour figurant sur ses armoiries, mais aussi par celle tout à fait fantasque qui domine les murs du jardin. Celui-ci, des plus charmants, est l'œuvre de plusieurs paysagistes talentueux, Luigi Cambray d'Igny, Gaetano Baccani et Bernardo Fallani, qui se succédèrent au début du XIXe siècle. Ce parc privé, le plus grand à être entouré d'une enceinte en Europe, renferme bien des secrets et trésors. Les vestiges des bastions de Florence datant de l'époque de Côme I (qui rejoignaient autrefois le Belvedere) se cachent sous d'antiques vignes-vierges, tandis que les sculptures et les allées attendent les amis de la famille, les artistes et les amateurs de parcs. Le *rondo* du jardin, construit autour d'une statue de Pietro Torrigiani et de son fils Luigi, est orienté avec précision d'après les quatre points cardinaux. Chaque saison est représentée par une allégorie.

El Palazzo o Casino Torrigiani del Campuccio es conocido no sólo por la torre de los escudos de armas que lo adornan, sino por la caprichosa atalaya visible por encima de los muros de la finca. Sus jardines, que invitan a la inspiración, fueron acondicionados a principios del siglo XIX sucesivamente por varios arquitectos, entre ellos Luigi Cambray d'Igny, Gaetano Baccani y Bernardo Fallani. En ninguna otra ciudad europea existe un jardín intramuros particular mayor que el de Torrigiani, que además acoge otros secretos y tesoros. Las ruinas de los muros florentinos de la época de Cosme I (que anteriormente llegaban hasta la fortaleza Belvedere) quedan cubiertas bajo las parras, mientras que sus esculturas y sendas atraen a amigos de la familia, artistas y amantes de los jardines. El *rondo* del jardín, construido alrededor de la estatua de Pietro Torrigiani y su hijo Luigi, se abre a las cuatro direcciones con otras tantas estatuas que representan las estaciones del año.

Fireplace with painting of Cardinale Marchese Luigi Torrigiani from Vico d'Elsa. A view into the dining room (the former "culture" room) from the salon.

Camino con dipinto *del cardinale marchese Luigi Torrigiani di Vico d'Elsa. Vista della sala da pranzo (un tempo salotto da conversazione) dal salone.*

Kamin mit einem *Bildnis von Kardinal Marchese Luigi Torrigiani von Vico d'Elsa. Blick vom Salon in das Esszimmer (das frühere Konversationszimmer).*

Une cheminée avec *un tableau du cardinal-marquis Luigi Torrigiani de Vico d'Elsa. Vue sur la salle à manger (ancienne salle de « culture »), depuis le salon.*

Chimenea con un *retrato del cardenal marqués Luigi Torrigiani de Vico d'Elsa. Vista del comedor (antigua sala de "cultura") desde el salón.*

The house and garden's location, in addition to having defined Florence's boundary under Cosimo I, has a storied past. During Roman times, the road linked Spain and the south of France to Rome, and *Pellegrini* would traverse it on their sacred sojourns to see the Pope. Medieval and Renaissance times witnessed the road's importance as a commercial route between Florence and Siena.

Il luogo in cui sorge il palazzo ha un passato carico di storia, oltre ad aver costituito il confine di Firenze all'epoca di Cosimo I. In epoca romana vi passava una strada che collegava la Spagna e il Sud della Francia a Roma, ed era percorsa dai pellegrini che, spinti dalla fede, si incamminavano per chiedere udienza al Papa; nel medioevo e nel rinascimento essa si trasformò in un'importante rotta commerciale tra Firenze e Siena.

Die Lage des Hauses und Gartens markierten nicht nur die Grenzlinie der Stadt Florenz unter Cosimo I., sondern weisen auch unabhängig davon eine geschichtsträchtige Vergangenheit auf. Zu Zeiten der antiken Römer verband die Straße Rom mit Spanien und dem Süden Frankreichs, während sie später von Pilgern für deren Weg zum Papst genutzt wurde. Im Mittelalter und in der Renaissance erreichte die Straße außerdem eine große Bedeutung als wichtige Handelsroute zwischen Florenz und Siena.

L'emplacement de la demeure et de son parc, qui a défini les limites de Florence sous Côme I, possède par ailleurs un passé chargé d'histoire. Autrefois, la route reliait l'Espagne et le sud de la France à Rome et les pèlerins l'empruntaient lors de leur périple vers la ville éternelle. Au Moyen Âge et à la Renaissance, elle devint une voie commerciale majeure entre Florence et Sienne.

El lugar de emplazamiento de la casa y los jardines, además de haber definido los límites de Florencia en tiempos de Cosme I, puede presumir de un rico pasado. En la época de los romanos, pasaba por allí la ruta que unía la península Ibérica y el sur de la Galia con Roma; posteriormente los peregrinos usaron esa misma senda en sus sagrados viajes para ver al Papa. Asimismo durante la Edad Media y el Renacimiento, el camino fue una importante ruta comercial entre Florencia y Siena.

Eleonora Torrigiani, daughter of Raffaele and Elena, with her grandfather General Giuseppe Torrigiani, the cavalry officer who wrote "Africa, Diary of War," detailing some of Italy's campaigns during World War II.

Eleonora Torrigiani figlia di Raffaele ed Elena, con il nonno, il generale Giuseppe Torrigiani, ufficiale di cavalleria autore di "Africa, diari di guerra", sulle campagne d'Africa della seconda guerra mondiale.

Eleonora Torrigiani, Tochter von Raffaele und Elena Torrigiani, und ihr Großvater, Kavalleriegeneral Giuseppe Torrigiani, der „Afrika – Ein Kriegstagebuch" verfasste und darin einige der italienischen Feldzüge während des Zweiten Weltkriegs schildert.

Eleonora Torrigiani, fille de Raffaele et d'Elena, avec son grand-père Giuseppe Torrigiani, le général de cavalerie qui écrivit « Afrique, Journal de guerre » en train d'étudier certaines des campagnes que mena l'Italie pendant la Seconde Guerre mondiale.

Eleonora Torrigiani, hija de Raffaele y Elena, con su abuelo Giuseppe Torrigiani, general de caballería que escribió "Africa, diario de guerra", en el que relata las campañas de Italia durante la Segunda Guerra Mundial.

Raffaele and Elena Torrigiani and family divide their time between this Florence home and the country farm, where Raffaele continues in the family's winemaking tradition. One ancestor, Ciardo Torrigiani, in the late 13th century, started a hotel and cellar in Florence; winemaking continues to this day.

Raffaele ed Elena Torrigiani, insieme alla famiglia, dividono il proprio tempo tra il palazzo fiorentino e l'azienda fuori città, dove Raffaele tiene alto il buon nome dei vini del casato. Ciardo Torrigiani, uno dei suoi antenati, aprì infatti una locanda con cantina a Firenze, sul finire del XIII secolo, dando il via a una tradizione che continua ancor oggi.

Raffaele und Elena Torrigiani und ihre Familie halten sich meist entweder in ihrem florentinischen Anwesen oder auf ihrem Landgut auf, wo der Hausherr immer noch der Familientradition folgt und Wein herstellt. Einer seiner Vorfahren, Ciardo Torrigiani, führte bereits im späten 13. Jahrhundert in Florenz eine Herberge und einen eigenen Weinkeller – eine Tradition, die sich bis heute gehalten hat.

Raffaele et Elena Torrigiani, ainsi que leur famille, partagent leur temps entre cette résidence florentine et leur exploitation agricole où Raffaele perpétue la tradition viticole de la famille. À la fin du XIIIᵉ siècle, l'un de leurs ancêtres, Ciardo Torrigiani, se lança dans l'hôtellerie et le commerce du vin à Florence ; la viticulture s'est maintenue jusqu'à ce jour.

Raffaele, Elena Torrigiani y su familia dividen el tiempo entre su hogar florentino y esta residencia campestre, donde Raffaele continúa con la tradición vitivinícola del clan. Uno de sus antepasados, Ciardo Torrigiani, inauguró a finales del siglo XIII un hotel y una bodega en Florencia; la explotación vinícola ha sobrevivido hasta hoy.

Statue: a baroque depiction of Actaeon, the mythological figure who was turned into a deer by Diana after she found him spying on her. The garden and palace, viewed from the tower.

Statua barocca raffigurante Atteone, il personaggio mitologico trasformato in cervo da Diana, che l'aveva sorpreso a spiarla. Il giardino e il palazzo visti dalla torre.

Barocke Statue des Aktaion, der von der Göttin Diana in einen Hirsch verwandelt wurde, nachdem er sie beim Baden beobachtet hatte. Park und Palast, vom Turm aus gesehen.

Statue : représentation baroque d'Actéon, le personnage mythologique que Diane transforma en cerf pour le punir de l'avoir observée en cachette. Le jardin et le palais, vus de la tour.

Estatua: una representación barroca de la figura mítica de Acteón, convertido en ciervo por Diana después de sorprenderlo espiándola. Jardín y palacio vistos desde la torre.

Corsini

Villa Le Corti, San Casciano Val di Pesa

The Corsini family has had a steady and significant impact on Italy and its culture for centuries. Among the family's ancestors, there are several of particular note. Saint Andrea (1302–1373) was born a Corsini in Florence, became a Carmelite monk and after his studies returned to his hometown as the "Apostle of Florence." He was sought out as a peacemaker, even being appointed as a personal representative of the Pope to heal relations in Bologna. He was canonized in 1629. Lorenzo Corsini, who originally studied law, became Pope Clement XII at the age of 78 in 1730. He lost his sight in his second year, but still managed to restore the papal finances in order, resurrect the public lottery, commission the Trevi fountain, pave the streets of Rome and the roads leading out of the city, begin the façade of St. John Lateran (where he was eventually buried) and build in that basilica the chapel of his ancestor, Saint Andrea.

La famiglia Corsini ha avuto un'influenza costante e significativa sull'Italia e la sua cultura nel corso dei secoli. Tra i suoi antenati vanta molti nomi illustri. Il famoso Sant'Andrea (1302–1373), per esempio, era un Corsini. Nacque a Firenze, entrò nell'ordine dei monaci carmelitani e, dopo aver terminato gli studi, tornò nella città natale come "apostolo di Firenze". Veniva spesso interpellato in qualità di mediatore, e fu addirittura nominato legato pontificio per le relazioni diplomatiche con Bologna. Fu proclamato santo nel 1629. Lorenzo Corsini, che aveva studiato legge, divenne invece Papa Clemente XII all'età di 78 anni, nel 1730. Pur perdendo la vista nel suo secondo anno di pontificato, riuscì ugualmente a risanare le finanze pontificie, a reintrodurre la lotteria, a commissionare la fontana di Trevi, a far pavimentare le strade di Roma e le vie che portavano fuori dalla città, a iniziare i lavori per la facciata della basilica di San Giovanni in Laterano (dove venne in seguito seppellito) e a farvi costruire la cappella per il suo antenato Sant'Andrea.

Die Familie Corsini übt seit vielen Jahrhunderten einen stetigen und bedeutenden Einfluss auf Italien und seine Kultur aus. Unter den Vorfahren der Familie gibt es eine ganze Anzahl großer Persönlichkeiten. So zum Beispiel den Heiligen Andrea (1302–1373), der ein geborener Corsini aus Florenz war, ehe er den Karmelitern beitrat, um schließlich nach seinen Lehrjahren als „Apostel von Florenz" in seine Heimatstadt zurückzukehren. Er wurde ein viel gerühmter Friedensstifter und in dieser Funktion sogar zum persönlichen Gesandten des Papstes ernannt, dessen Beziehungen zu Bologna er wiederherzustellen hatte. 1629 wurde Andrea heilig gesprochen. Lorenzo Corsini hingegen, der ursprünglich Rechtswissenschaften studiert hatte, wurde im Alter von 78 Jahren 1730 zum Papst Clemens XII. gewählt. In seinem zweiten Amtsjahr verlor er das Augenlicht, was ihn aber nicht daran hinderte, die päpstlichen Finanzen zu konsolidieren, die öffentliche Lotterie erneut ins Leben zu rufen, den Auftrag für den Bau des Trevi-Brunnens zu erteilen, die Straßen von Rom sowie die Ausfallstraßen pflastern zu lassen und mit dem Bau der Fassade der Lateransbasilika zu beginnen (wo er schließlich auch seine letzte Ruhe fand). Dort ließ er auch eine Kapelle für seinen Ahnen, den Heiligen Andrea, errichten.

La famille Corsini exerce une influence continue et significative sur l'Italie et sa culture depuis des siècles. Plusieurs de ses ancêtres se sont distingués de façon particulière. Saint André (1302–1373), un Corsini, naquit à Florence avant de devenir carmélite et de revenir, une fois ses études achevées, dans sa ville natale comme « l'apôtre de Florence ». Les gens venaient le chercher pour qu'il règle les litiges et il fut même nommé légat du pape pour apaiser les relations avec Bologne. Il fut canonisé en 1629. Lorenzo Corsini, qui avait étudié le droit, devint pape sous le nom de Clément XII à l'âge de 78 ans, en 1730. Il perdit la vue pendant la deuxième année de son pontificat, mais réussit néanmoins à remettre de l'ordre dans les finances papales, à ressusciter la loterie, à commanditer la fontaine de Trévi, à paver les rues de Rome et les routes d'accès et à commencer la façade de Saint-Jean de Latran (où il fut inhumé). Enfin, il éleva dans cette basilique une chapelle à son ancêtre, saint André.

La familia Corsini ha tenido una constante y significativa influencia en la historia y la cultura italiana durante siglos. El clan cuenta con varios antepasados destacados. San Andrea (1302–1373), nacido en Florencia con el apellido Corsini, se hizo monje carmelita. Tras finalizar los estudios retornó a su ciudad natal convertido en el "apóstol de Florencia". Fue muy apreciado como mediador de paz y llegó a ser nombrado representante del Papa para intentar reestablecer las relaciones con Bolonia. Fue canonizado en 1629. Lorenzo Corsini, que en un principio estudió leyes, llegó a convertirse en el Papa Clemente XII en 1730 a la edad de setenta y ocho años. Aunque perdió la vista dos años después, logró sanear las finanzas pontificias, reinstauró la lotería pública, encargó la Fontana de Trevi, pavimentó las calles de Roma y las carreteras que conducían a la ciudad, inició los trabajos de construcción de la fachada de San Juan Laterano (donde posteriormente sería enterrado) y acondicionó en dicha basílica una capilla en memoria de su antepasado san Andrea.

Two villa bedrooms with appealingly different character: Empire bed with bearskin rug and a trompe l'œil window surround framing the Tuscan view.

Diverso carattere di due camere da letto della villa: letto Impero con tappeto di pelle d'orso e finestra con trompe l'œil a incorniciare la vista sul paesaggio toscano.

Zwei Schlafgemächer der Villa mit unterschiedlichem Ambiente: ein Empire-Bett mit Bärenfell und eine Trompe-l'Œil-Fensterumrandung, der eine toskanische Aussicht einrahmt.

Deux chambres à coucher de la villa aux caractères agréablement différents : lit Empire, descente de lit en peau d'ours, et fenêtre en trompe-l'œil encadrant une vue de la Toscane.

Dos alcobas de la villa con un carácter diferente y atractivo: cama estilo Imperio con alfombra de oso y ventana con trompe l'œil que enmarca el paisaje toscano.

The "Wedding Room" *is a painted record of the families that have married into the Corsini clan. Duccio's own "clan" includes wife Clotilde and children Filippo and Elena.*

La "Stanza dei matrimoni" *con la testimonianza pittorica delle famiglie entrate a far parte dei Corsini per matrimonio. La famiglia di Duccio comprende la moglie Clotilde e i figli Filippo ed Elena.*

Im „Hochzeitszimmer" *wurde malerisch festgehalten, wer in das Geschlecht der Corsini einheiratete. Zu Duccio Corsinis enger Familie gehören seine Frau Clotilde und die Kinder Filippo und Elena.*

La « Salle des mariages » *évoque en peinture les familles qui se sont alliées au clan Corsini. Le propre clan de Duccio comprend son épouse Clotilde, ainsi que leurs enfants Filippo et Elena.*

La "Alcoba nupcial" *es un registro pintado de los escudos de armas de las familias que han emparentado por matrimonio con los Corsini. El clan de Duccio está formado por su esposa Clotilde y los hijos, Filippo y Elena.*

Diego Paternò Castello di San Guiliano, Duccio's brother-in-law, with his daughter Fabiola in the Carmine Church, where Saint Andrea is buried. Altar and crucifix of the private Le Corti chapel.

Diego Paternò Castello di San Giuliano, cognato di Duccio, con la figlia Fabiola nella chiesa del Carmine, dove è sepolto Sant'Andrea. Altare e crocefisso della cappella privata della Villa Le Corti.

Diego Paternò Castello di San Guiliano, der Schwager Duccio Corsinis, mit seiner Tochter Fabiola in der Carmine-Kirche, wo der Heilige Andrea begraben liegt. Altar und Kruzifix der privaten Le-Corti-Kapelle.

Diego Paternò Castello di San Guiliano (le beau-frère de Duccio) avec sa fille Fabiola à l'église du Carmine, où est enterré saint André. Autel et crucifix de la chapelle privée Le Corti.

Diego Paternò Castello di San Guiliano (cuñado de Duccio) con su hija Fabiola en la iglesia de Carmine, en la que está sepultado San Andrea. Altar y crucifijo de la capilla particular de Le Corti.

A salon's extensive trompe l'œil of balustrades, vines and flower pots together with its antique bird cage collection, fountain and light furniture create an outdoor effect.

In una sala il grande trompe l'œil con balaustre, viti e vasi di fiori, la collezione di antiche gabbie per uccelli, la fontana e l'arredamento leggero danno la sensazione di trovarsi in mezzo alla natura.

Ein aufwendiges Trompe-l'Œil mit Balustraden, Weinranken und Blumentöpfen sowie eine Sammlung alter Vogelkäfige, ein Springbrunnen und helle Möbel verleihen diesem Salon den Anschein, als würde man sich im Freien befinden.

Les peintures en tromp-l'œil du salon, représentant des balustrades, des vignes et des pots de fleurs, ainsi que la collection de cages d'oiseaux anciennes, la fontaine et le mobilier léger, donnent l'impression d'être en plein air.

La decoración del salón con un trompe l'œil de balaustradas y motivos de parras y macetas con flores, así como una colección de jaulas antiguas, la fuente y el ligero mobiliario crean un efecto de espacio al aire libre.

The Corsinis continue to contribute to and enhance culture today. Palazzo Corsini hosts an international antiques fair each fall, as well as a fair for artisans each spring. South of Florence, nestled in the heart of Chianti, the family of Duccio Corsini is working to restore another piece of Tuscan history, Villa Le Corti. The Corsini have owned the Villa since its first role in 1427 as part of Florence's defense line; it was converted to a home in the early 1600s. The family has been working to reinvigorate the vines and the olive trees that are the traditional landscape of Tuscany, as well as restoring the Villa's exterior and interiors. The Villa's chapel is ornamented with 17th century frescoes, as well as a family history of coats of arms painted on the walls and ceiling of the "wedding room." In addition to the work to the physical estate, the family hosts cultural events, such as the "Giardini in Fiera," an annual garden fair in September, which includes landscaping conferences, held in the Villa and Italianate garden. In the spring, Le Corti hosts "Alla Corte del Vino," a wine fair and tasting of major Tuscan wine producers.

A tutt'oggi il contributo dei Corsini al mondo della cultura è significativo. In autunno il Palazzo Corsini ospita una fiera internazionale di antiquariato, mentre in primavera una fiera di artigianato. La famiglia di Duccio Corsini, inoltre, è responsabile del recupero di un altro dei tanti pezzi di storia della Toscana annidato nel cuore del Chianti, a sud di Firenze: Villa Le Corti. I Corsini sono stati i padroni della villa sin dal 1427, quando era una semplice fortificazione della linea difensiva di Firenze. Venne convertita in abitazione civile agli albori del XVII secolo. La famiglia si è adoperata per rinvigorirne le vigne e gli uliveti, simbolo del paesaggio toscano, ma anche per ristrutturarne sia gli interni che l'esterno. La cappella della Villa è decorata con affreschi del XVII secolo, mentre i vari stemmi araldici del casato nei secoli decorano le mura e il soffitto della cosiddetta "stanza dei matrimoni". I Corsini non si sono però limitati soltanto a ristrutturare la proprietà, ma hanno organizzato eventi culturali ospitati nella villa e nel suo giardino all'italiana: tra questi "Giardini in fiera", mostra annuale di cultura del giardino che si tiene a settembre con molte conferenze sul paesaggio, e "Alla corte del vino", una fiera primaverile con degustazioni enogastronomiche a cui partecipano i più grandi produttori della Toscana.

Die Corsini fördern heute noch die Kultur ihrer Stadt und die des Landes. Im Palazzo Corsini findet jeden Herbst eine internationale Antiquitätenmesse und im Frühjahr eine Kunsthandwerkermesse statt. Südlich von Florenz, mitten im Herzen des Chianti-Landstrichs, ist die Familie von Duccio Corsini damit beschäftigt, ein Stück toskanischer Geschichte zu restaurieren – die Villa Le Corti. Das Geschlecht der Corsini besitzt diese Villa seit 1427, als diese zum Verteidigungsring der Stadt Florenz gehörte. Die Villa wurde dann im frühen 17. Jahrhundert so umgebaut, dass man auch darin wohnen konnte. Heute bemüht sich die Familie, die Rebstöcke und Olivenbäume, die zur traditionellen Landschaft der Toskana gehören, wieder neu anzupflanzen und zugleich das Äußere und das Innere des Gebäudes zu restaurieren. In der Kapelle des Anwesens finden sich Fresken aus dem 17. Jahrhundert, und das Familienwappen schmückt Wände und die Decke des „Hochzeitssaals". Abgesehen von den Restaurierungsarbeiten, veranstaltet die Familie wichtige kulturelle Ereignisse wie die „Giardini in Fiera", eine jährliche Gartenmesse im September. Dazu gehören u. a. verschiedene Konferenzen zur Landschaftsarchitektur, die in der Villa und in ihrem kunstvoll angelegten Garten abgehalten werden. Im Frühling hingegen versammeln sich alle großen Weinproduzenten der Toskana zur alljährlichen Weinmesse „Alla Corte del Vino".

Aujourd'hui encore, les Corsini apportent une importante contribution dans le domaine culturel. Le palais Corsini accueille un salon international d'antiquités chaque automne, ainsi qu'une foire d'artisanat au printemps. Au sud de Florence, en plein cœur du Chianti, la famille de Duccio Corsini œuvre à la restauration d'un autre pan de l'histoire florentine, la Villa Le Corti. Les Corsini en sont les propriétaires depuis 1427, lorsqu'elle se distingua pour la première fois par son appartenance à la ligne de défense de Florence ; elle fut convertie en demeure au début du XVIIᵉ siècle. La famille s'est consacrée à faire revivre les vignes et les oliveraies qui constituent le paysage traditionnel de la Toscane, mais a aussi restauré les extérieurs et les intérieurs de la villa. Sa chapelle est ornée de fresques du XVIIᵉ siècle, de même que d'un historique des armoiries de la famille, peint sur les murs et le plafond de la « salle nuptiale ». Outre les travaux d'entretien, la famille organise divers événements culturels, tels que les « Giardini in Fiera », un salon d'horticulture qui se tient chaque année en septembre et propose des conférences sur le paysagisme ayant lieu dans la villa et les jardins à l'italienne. Au printemps, Le Corti accueille « Alla Corte del Vino », une foire aux vins où les visiteurs peuvent déguster les produits des principaux viticulteurs toscans.

En la actualidad, los Corsini siguen contribuyendo y fomentando la cultura. El palacio que lleva su nombre acoge en otoño una feria de antigüedades y en primavera una muestra de arte. Al sur de Florencia, en pleno corazón de la Toscana, la familia de Duccio Corsini trabaja para restaurar otra pieza de la historia de la región: Villa Le Corti. El clan ha sido propietario de la finca desde 1427, cuando formaba parte de las líneas defensivas de Florencia. La casona se convirtió en su residencia en el siglo XVII. La familia ha invertido mucho esfuerzo en recuperar los viñedos y olivares característicos del paisaje toscano, así como en restaurar la villa por dentro y por fuera. La capilla de la mansión está ornamentada con frescos del siglo XVII y con la historia del linaje ilustrada en escudos de armas pintados en las paredes y en el techo de la "sala nupcial". Además de dedicarse a la reestructuración de la hacienda, los Corsini organizan eventos culturales como la llamada "Giardini in Fiera" o feria de jardinería celebrada todos los años en septiembre, durante la que se dan conferencias sobre arquitectura de paisajes en el marco de la villa y sus jardines italianizantes. En primavera, Le Corti acoge "Alla Corte del Vino", una feria en la que se pueden degustar los caldos de los productores toscanos más relevantes.

*Elena and **Filippo Corsini** and Luca Guicciardini Corsi Salviati at a pheasant hunt on the Renacci Estate.*

*Elena e **Filippo Corsini** con Luca Guicciardini Corsi Salviati a una caccia al fagiano presso la tenuta di Renacci.*

*Elena und **Filippo Corsini** sowie Luca Guicciardini Corsi Salviati bei einer Fasanenjagd auf dem Anwesen von Renacci.*

*Elena et **Filippo Corsini** et Luca Guicciardini Corsi Salviati lors d'une chasse au faisan sur la propriété de Renacci.*

*Elena y **Filippo Corsini**, y Luca Guicciardini Corsi Salviati cazando faisanes en la hacienda de Renacci.*

Venerosi Pesciolini

Tenuta di Ghizzano, Peccioli

Midway between Pisa and Florence, nestled into the *Colline Pisane* (Hills of Pisa) the Ghizzano Estate has been in the Venerosi Pesciolini family since 1370. The home's rooms radiate the intimate coziness of family life. The two-story *Galleria* exhibits past generations; paintings and drawings of family and friends are interspersed with art books and the house's ancestral furniture. For centuries, the family viewed the country estate as a pleasant location for repose and recreation, and the estate's tending followed historical, traditional practices; the way things had always been done created a template for its future.

La tenuta di Ghizzano, appollaiata sui colli pisani a metà strada tra Pisa e Firenze, appartiene alla famiglia Venerosi Pesciolini sin dal 1370. Le sale della magione trasmettono tutto il calore di un'accogliente ambiente familiare. All'interno della sua galleria a due piani le generazioni passate fanno mostra di sé, e i ritratti di familiari e amici si mescolano ai libri d'arte e ai mobili appartenuti agli avi del casato. Per secoli la famiglia ha considerato questa tenuta di campagna come un semplice luogo di riposo e di piacere, ed è sempre stata gestita seguendo antiche pratiche di consolidata tradizione. Sul riconoscimento del passato è fondato il futuro di questa azienda.

Zwischen Pisa und Florenz liegt mitten in den *Colline Pisane* (den Hügeln von Pisa) der Landsitz Ghizzano, welcher seit 1370 der Familie Venerosi Pesciolini gehört. Die Räume des Hauses strahlen die intime Atmosphäre eines engen Familienlebens aus. In der zweigeschossigen Galerie können die Vorfahren betrachtet werden: Gemälde und Zeichnungen der Familie und von Freunden befinden sich inmitten ererbter Möbelstücke und zahlreicher Kunstbände. Jahrhundertelang verstand die Familie den Landsitz als einen angenehmen Ort der Entspannung und Erholung, und die Bewirtschaftung der Ländereien folgte historisch gewachsenen, traditionellen Mustern. Was man und wie man etwas früher einmal machte, diente als Vorlage für die Zukunft.

À mi-chemin entre Pise et Florence et nichée dans les *Colline Pisane* (collines de Pise), la villa Ghizzano appartient à la famille Venerosi Pesciolini depuis 1370. Un confort intime de vie familiale émane des pièces de cette demeure. La *Galleria* qui occupe deux étages est remplie des témoignages des générations passées ; les tableaux et les dessins de la famille et des amis y côtoient livres d'art et mobilier ancestral. Pendant des siècles, la famille a considéré la propriété comme un lieu agréable pour se reposer et se divertir, et l'a gérée selon des pratiques historiques et traditionnelles, qui tenaient lieu de modèle pour l'avenir.

A medio camino entre Pisa y Florencia y bien resguardada por las *Colline Pisane* (colinas de Pisa) se encuentra la estancia Ghizzano, residencia de la familia Venerosi Pesciolini desde 1370. Las piezas de esta propiedad irradian la acogedora intimidad de la vida familiar. La galería de dos pisos exhibe vestigios de pasadas generaciones: pinturas y dibujos de familiares y amigos se alternan con libros de arte y el ancestral mobiliario de la casa. Durante siglos, la familia ha disfrutado de esta residencia campestre como apacible lugar de descanso y recreo. Por otro lado, el mantenimiento de las tierras se ha llevado a cabo siguiendo prácticas históricas y tradicionales; la forma en la que se han hecho siempre las cosas ha creado un precedente y un ejemplo de futuro.

Painting and sketches by 20th century Italian painter Pietro Annigoni. The galleria's transom, or fanlight, affords a view of the ceiling of the entryway pergola.

Dipinti e schizzi di Pietro Annigoni, pittore italiano del XX secolo. Dalla lunetta della galleria si scorge la pergola dipinta sul soffitto del vestibolo.

Gemälde und Skizzen des italienischen Malers Pietro Annigoni aus dem 20. Jahrhundert. Vom Oberlicht der Galerie aus hat man einen wunderbaren Blick auf die Eingangs-Pergola.

Peintures et dessins du peintre italien Pietro Annigoni (XXe siècle). On aperçoit à travers l'imposte de la galerie le haut de la pergola.

Pinturas y bocetos del siglo XX del pintor italiano Pietro Annigoni. El dintel o montante de abanico permite ver el techo de la entrada con decoración de pérgola.

Armed with the belief that the estate could benefit from progressive agricultural practices and even produce fine wines, recent generations have injected the time-worn practices of the estate with cutting edge techniques. The vineyards have been invigorated and farming practices reinvented. Though winemaking had been a part of the estate for centuries, the wine's increasing reputation is attributable to the modern, tireless efforts first of Count Pierfrancesco Venerosi Pesciolini and his wife Carla, and currently by daughters Lisa and Ginevra.

Le generazioni più recenti della famiglia, convinte che la tenuta avrebbe tratto giovamento dall'introduzione di tecniche agricole più al passo coi tempi e dalla produzione di vini di qualità, hanno cercato di rivoluzionare l'azienda, rinvigorendo le vigne e sostituendo metodi ormai vetusti con tecniche agricole all'avanguardia. Anche se il vino è stato prodotto per secoli in questa tenuta, il prestigio sempre maggiore che viene attribuito alle sue uve è merito soprattutto degli sforzi e delle innovazioni introdotte dal conte Pierfrancesco Venerosi Pesciolini e sua moglie Carla nonché, attualmente, dalle figlie Lisa e Ginevra.

Im festen Glauben, dass das Landgut von fortschrittlichen Landwirtschaftspraktiken profitieren und gute Weine hervorbringen könnte, haben die jüngeren Generationen der Familie die altvertrauten Methoden durch neueste Techniken verbessert. Die Weinberge wurden zu neuem Leben erweckt und die landwirtschaftliche Bewirtschaftung neu strukturiert. Obwohl die Herstellung von Wein hier seit Jahrhunderten betrieben wird, ist der zunehmend gute Ruf der Weine auf die starken Bemühungen des Grafen Pierfrancesco Venerosi Pesciolini und seiner Frau Carla und in jüngerer Zeit ihrer Töchter Lisa und Ginevra zurückzuführen.

Les générations récentes, convaincues que le domaine pouvait tirer parti des avancées en matière d'agriculture et même produire des vins de qualité, ont supplanté ces pratiques dépassées par des techniques de pointe. Elles ont ressuscité les vignes et réinventé les pratiques agricoles. Si la viticulture est restée indissociable de la propriété pendant des siècles, la réputation croissante des vins est le fruit des efforts incessants du comte Pierfrancesco Venerosi Pesciolini et de son épouse Carla, et aujourd'hui de leurs filles Lisa et Ginevra.

Plenamente convencidas de que la finca puede beneficiarse de los métodos de explotación agrícolas más modernos e incluso llegar a producir excelentes vinos, las nuevas generaciones han injertado las inmemoriales prácticas de la estancia con las técnicas más punteras; se han mejorado las cepas y reestructurado la explotación agrícola. Aunque la vitivinicultura ha sido parte de la vida de la finca desde hace siglos, la creciente reputación de su vino debe atribuirse en primer lugar a los modernos e incansables esfuerzos del conde Pierfrancesco Venerosi Pesciolini y su esposa Carla y, más actualmente, de sus hijas Lisa y Ginevra.

With a background in publishing, and a degree in language and literature, Ginevra moved from a career of books to immersing herself in the land in the 1990s. She applied her attention to detail to the land, from the planting of the vines to the enology in the cellar, and has been working the wine on the estate full time since 1996. Her philosophy centers on protecting and honoring the spirit of her ancestors' traditions through innovative strategies and techniques. To that end, the whole farm utilizes organic practices, and is supporting the development of biological energy, particularly to create sustainable energy to run the estate. Ginevra currently serves as the president of the Association of the Grand Cru wines of Coastal Tuscany.

Proprio Ginevra, laureata in lettere, dopo aver lavorato nel campo dell'editoria, negli anni 1990 ha abbandonato i libri per dedicarsi esclusivamente alla terra. Ha applicato il suo gusto per i dettagli all'attività di famiglia, dalla semina delle vigne alla conservazione dei vini, e dal 1996 cura a tempo pieno la produzione della tenuta. La filosofia da lei seguita si basa sul rispetto e la salvaguardia delle tradizioni dei suoi antenati e sull'introduzione di strategie e tecnologie innovative. A questo scopo l'azienda pratica l'agricoltura biologica e ha adottato fonti di energia ecologiche, che le permettono di ottenere tutto il fabbisogno necessario in maniera sostenibile. Ginevra è l'attuale presidente dell'associazione Grandi cru della Costa Toscana.

Ginevra, die Sprachen und Literatur studierte und ursprünglich in der Verlagsbranche tätig war, wechselte in den 1990er-Jahren von der Welt der Bücher zu der des Weins. Ihr Aufgabenbereich betrifft die vielen Details, die mit der Weinherstellung einhergehen – vom Pflanzen der Weinreben bis zur richtigen Lagerung im Keller. Seit 1996 arbeitet sie ausschließlich auf dem Gut. Ihre Philosophie ist es, den Geist ihrer Vorfahren gerade dadurch zu bewahren und zu ehren, indem sie innovative Strategien und Techniken anwendet. So wird auf dem ganzen Gut biologisch gewirtschaftet und die Entwicklung alternativer Energien tatkräftig unterstützt, um u. a. damit das Gut selbst zu versorgen. Ginevra Venerosi Pesciolini steht zudem augenblicklich der Gesellschaft der Grand-Cru-Weine der toskanischen Küste vor.

Ginevra, diplômée de langues et de littérature, débuta dans l'édition avant d'abandonner les livres pour se consacrer au domaine dans les années 1990. Accordant une attention particulière au terroir, à la plantation des ceps, à l'œnologie et aux chais, elle travaille à plein temps dans l'exploitation viticole depuis 1996. Pour elle, les stratégies et les techniques novatrices permettent de rendre hommage à l'esprit de ses ancêtres et à leurs traditions. Dans ce but, le domaine tout entier applique des techniques biologiques et soutient le développement des énergies bio, en particulier pour créer une énergie durable servant à l'exploitation. Ginevra est actuellement présidente de l'Association des vins de grand cru de la côte toscane.

Con gran experiencia en el mundo editorial y una licenciatura en Lengua y Literatura, Ginevra cambió el mundo de los libros por el del campo en la década de 1990, cuando decidió abocar su atención a las actividades familiares y cuidar de los más pequeños detalles, desde la plantación de las cepas hasta la labor enológica en la bodega. Así se ha dedicado en cuerpo y alma a elaborar el vino de esta hacienda desde 1996. Su filosofía se centra en conservar y honrar el espíritu de la tradición de sus ancestros sin renunciar por ello a estrategias y técnicas innovadoras. Con este fin, en la hacienda se utilizan métodos orgánicos y se apoya el desarrollo de energía, en especial aquella que permita cubrir las necesidades de la estancia. En la actualidad, Ginevra es la presidenta de la Associazione Grandi Cru della Costa Toscana.

The family's coat of arms contains a symbol of a fish, thus evoking the name Pesciolini (little fish). The gate and stairway to the house lead up from the estate's extensive gardens.

Lo stemma della famiglia raffigura un pesce, in assonanza con il nome Pesciolini. Ingresso e scalinata che dagli ampi giardini della tenuta conducono alla casa.

Im Familienwappen findet sich das Symbol des Fisches, das auf den Namen Pesciolini (kleiner Fisch) anspielt. Von den ausgedehnten Gärten des Anwesens führen Tor und Treppe zum Haus.

Le blason de la famille a pour symbole un poisson évoquant le nom de Pesciolini (petit poisson). Le portail et l'escalier assurent la transition entre le vaste parc et la demeure.

El escudo de armas de la familia muestra el símbolo de un pez, en alusión al apellido Pesciolini (pececito). El portón y las escaleras que conducen a la casa desde los enormes jardines de la estancia.

Capponi

Palazzo Capponi, Firenze

The Capponi family has been influential in Florence from the mid 13th century, helping shape the silk trade, banking, politics and its intellectual life for centuries. Lodovico Capponi (1482–1534) was banker to Popes Leo X and Clement VII. He commissioned the Capponi Chapel at *Santa Felicita*, and was patron to painter Jacopo Pontormo. Marquis Gino Capponi (1792–1876) was an ardent Anglophile, and founded the *Antologia*, inspired by the literary *Edinburgh Review* before turning his attention to politics (though totally blind by 1844, he served briefly as Prime Minister in 1848, was elected to the Tuscan assembly in 1859, and was made senator in 1860). Another of his many accomplishments was his devotion to sacred and secular history—among his works is *Storia della Repubblica di Firenze* (History of the Republic of Florence).

A partire dalla metà del XIII secolo quella dei Capponi è stata una famiglie più influenti di Firenze: ha contribuito ad avviarne il commercio della seta e per secoli ha plasmato la vita economica, politica e culturale della città. Lodovico Capponi (1482–1534) fu il banchiere dei papi Leone X e Clemente VII. Commissionò la Cappella Capponi a Santa Felicita e fu mecenate del pittore Jacopo Pontormo. Il marchese Gino Capponi (1792–1876), fervente anglofilo, fondò la rivista letteraria *Antologia*, sul modello dell'*Edinburgh Review*, per poi dedicarsi alla politica. Anche se già nel 1844 era ormai completamente privo della vista, infatti, ricoprì brevemente la carica di primo ministro nel 1848, diventò membro dell'Assemblea dei rappresentanti della Toscana nel 1859 e senatore nel 1860. Uno dei suoi numerosi interessi degni di nota era l'amore per la storia sia religiosa che politica, che lo portò a scrivere *Storia della Repubblica di Firenze*.

Die Familie Capponi spielt seit Mitte des 13. Jahrhunderts eine wichtige Rolle in der Geschichte der Stadt Florenz. Sie beeinflussten den Seidenhandel, das Bankwesen, die Politik und das intellektuelle Leben. Lodovico Capponi (1482–1534) war der Bankier der Päpste Leo X. und Clemens VII. Er gab den Auftrag für den Bau der Capponi-Kapelle in der Kirche *Santa Felicita* und war Mäzen des Malers Jacopo Pontormo. Sein Nachfahre, der Marquis Gino Capponi (1792–1876), galt als leidenschaftlich anglophil und gründete die Zeitschrift *Antologia*, die vom *Edinburgh Review* inspiriert wurde, ehe er sein Interesse der Politik zuwandte. Obwohl er bereits 1844 völlig erblindet war, hielt er 1848 vorübergehend den Posten als Premierminister inne, wurde 1859 ins toskanische Parlament gewählt und 1860 zum Senator ernannt. Außerdem galt seine Leidenschaft sowohl der sakralen als auch der säkularen Geschichte; er verfasste u. a. die *Storia della Repubblica di Firenze* (Geschichte der Republik Florenz).

La famille Capponi, qui a contribué pendant des siècles au développement de la soierie, de l'activité bancaire, de la politique et de la vie intellectuelle, fait sentir son influence à Florence depuis la moitié du XIIIe siècle. Lodovico Capponi (1482–1534) fut le banquier des papes Léon X et Clément VII. Il commandita la chapelle Capponi à *Santa Felicita* et fut un mécène du peintre Jacopo Pontormo. Anglophile convaincu, le marquis Gino Capponi (1792–1876) fonda la revue littéraire *Antologia*, sur le modèle de *l'Edinburgh Review*, avant de s'intéresser à la politique (bien que frappé de cécité complète en 1844, il fut brièvement premier ministre en 1848, fut élu à l'assemblée de la Toscane en 1859 et devint sénateur en 1860). Parmi ses nombreuses réalisations, citons sa passion pour l'histoire religieuse et séculaire, puisqu'il est l'auteur d'une *Storia della Repubblica di Firenze* (Histoire de la République de Florence).

La familia Capponi ha gozado de gran influencia en Florencia desde mediados del siglo XIII, contribuyendo durante largo tiempo al desarrollo del comercio de la seda, la banca y la vida política e intelectual. Lodovico Capponi (1482–1534) fue el banquero de los papas Leo X y Clemente VII. Él mandó construir la capilla Capponi en la iglesia de *Santa Felicita*, y fue el mecenas del pintor Jacopo Pontormo. El marqués Gino Capponi (1792–1876), ferviente anglófilo, fundó la publicación *Antologia*, inspirándose en la revista literaria *Edinburgh Review*. Más tarde se dedicó activamente a la política: aunque se quedó totalmente ciego en 1844, ejerció brevemente el cargo de primer ministro en 1848, fue elegido para formar parte de la asamblea toscana en 1859 y llegó a ser nombrado senador en 1860. Otro de sus muchos talentos fue la devoción por la historia sacra y secular, entre sus obras destaca el tratado *Storia della Repubblica di Firenze* (Historia de la Republicá de Florencia).

Details from the chapel *of the Palazzo Capponi: La Madonna Capponi by Jacopo Pontormo and bible.*

Particolari dalla cappella *di Palazzo Capponi: la Madonna con bambino del Jacopo Pontormo e Bibbia.*

Details der Kapelle *des Palazzo Capponi: das Gemälde La Madonna Capponi von Jacopo Pontormo und Bibel.*

Détails de la chapelle *du Palazzo Capponi : La Madonna Capponi, de Jacopo Pontormo, et une bible.*

Detalles de la capilla *del palacio Capponi: La Madonna Capponi, pintura de Jacopo Pontormo y biblia.*

The Gran Salone with the hanging tapestry containing the monogram of Count Ferrante Maria Capponi.

Il Gran Salone: i copriporte sono decorati con le iniziali del conte Ferrante Maria Capponi.

Der Gran Salone mit Vorhängen, auf denen die Initialen des Grafen Ferrante Maria Capponi zu sehen sind.

Le Gran Salone avec les tentures marquées des initiales du comte Ferrante Maria Capponi.

En el Gran Salone cuelgan cortinas con las iniciales del conde Ferrante Maria Capponi.

The Capponi palace was built by Niccolò da Uzzano in the early 15th century, and the courtyard is the first known example of a Renaissance courtyard. The palace's rooms are so large as to feel spare, though they are ornamented with details of the 600 years of family and civic history: the ancient family's coat of arms—a mismatched suit of armor (the top is 16th century, the bottom 15th)—and silks on the walls seem to hearken back to the Capponi's silk trade. The centerpiece of the palace's private chapel is a painting by Jacopo Pontormo—*La Madonna Capponi* is opposite the door of the chapel; light streams into the chapel through the 1526 stained glass window of Guillaume de Marcillat. More works by the painter and a copy of the window adorn the renowned Capponi Chapel in the Florentine church of *Santa Felicita*. The Palace played a role in modern filmmaking, serving as home and employer to the fictional Hannibal Lecter in the film *Hannibal*; Count Niccolò Capponi, professor and historian, aided Thomas Harris with research in the writing of the book, set in Florence.

Palazzo Capponi fu costruito da Niccolò da Uzzano agli inizi del XV secolo. Al suo interno è conservato il primo esempio riconosciuto di cortile rinascimentale. Le sale del palazzo sono tanto ampie da sembrare vuote, pur essendo arricchite dai simboli di più di 600 anni di storia familiare e civica: gli antichi stemmi araldici del casato, un'armatura completa, i cui pezzi risalgono però a epoche differenti (la parte superiore è del XVI secolo, quella inferiore del XV), la seta alla pareti che chiama alla memoria echi dell'antico commercio dei Capponi. Le opere di maggior rilievo della cappella privata del palazzo sono un dipinto di Jacopo Pontormo intitolato *Madonna con bambino*, situato esattamente di fronte alla porta di entrata, e la vetrata istoriata che dà luce all'ambiente, realizzata nel 1526 da Guillaume de Marcillat. Alcune altre opere del Pontormo, insieme a una copia della vetrata, adornano la famosa Cappella Capponi nella chiesa fiorentina di Santa Felicita. Il palazzo è entrato anche nella storia del cinema come dimora e ufficio del famoso Hannibal Lecter, nel film *Hannibal*. Il conte Niccolò Capponi, professore e storico, è stato consulente dello scrittore Thomas Harris per la parte del libro da cui è tratta la pellicola ambientata a Firenze.

Der Palazzo Capponi wurde von Niccolò da Uzzano im frühen 15. Jahrhundert erbaut, und sein Innenhof gilt als der erste, der im Geiste der Renaissance entstanden ist. Die Räumlichkeiten im Palast sind derart riesig, dass sie fast leer wirken, auch wenn sie mit zahlreichen Details aus 600 Jahren Familien- und Stadtgeschichte geschmückt sind. Man findet dort zum Beispiel das uralte Familienwappen, eine nicht zusammengehörige Ritterrüstung (der obere Teil stammt aus dem 16., der untere aus dem 15. Jahrhundert) sowie Seidenbehänge an den Wänden, die an den früheren Seidenhandel der Capponis erinnern. Das Herzstück der Privatkapelle im Palast bildet ein Gemälde von Jacopo Pontormo – *La Madonna Capponi* –, das sich dem Eingang gegenüber befindet. Tageslicht fällt durch ein Fenster des Künstlers Guillaume de Marcillat, das im Jahre 1526 entstand. Andere Gemälde des Malers und eine Kopie des Fensters zieren die berühmte Capponi-Kapelle in der Florentiner Kirche *Santa Felicita*. Der Palazzo ist auch in heutiger Zeit immer wieder gefragt – zuletzt als Filmkulisse für Hannibal Lecter's erfundenes Heim im Film *Hannibal*. Professor Graf Niccolò Capponi, ein Historiker, half Thomas Harris auch bei dessen Recherchearbeiten in der Stadt Florenz, als er den gleichnamigen Roman dort verfasste.

Au début du XVe siècle, Niccolò da Uzzano édifia le palais Capponi dont la cour est le premier exemple connu de style Renaissance. L'immensité des pièces donne l'impression qu'elles sont vides, alors qu'elles regorgent de souvenirs de 600 ans d'histoire familiale et publique : les anciennes armoiries de la famille, une armure dépareillée (le haut datant du XVIe et le bas du XVe) ou les tentures murales en soie qui évoquent l'activité des Capponi dans le commerce de la soie. Dans la chapelle privée, qui constitue la pièce maîtresse du palais, *La Madonnna Capponi*, peinte par Jacopo Pontormo, fait face à la porte. La lumière y entre par un vitrail de 1526, réalisé par Guillaume de Marcillat. Plusieurs autres œuvres de ce peintre, ainsi qu'une copie du vitrail, agrémentent la chapelle Capponi, joyau de l'église *Santa Felicita* à Florence. Le palais a joué un rôle dans le cinéma contemporain, puisqu'il a servi de demeure au personnage d'Hannibal Lecter dans le film *Hannibal* ; le comte Niccolò Capponi, professeur et historien, a aidé Thomas Harris dans ses recherches pour son livre, qui a pour cadre Florence.

El palacio Capponi fue levantado por Niccolò da Uzzano a principios del siglo XV y su patio renacentista es el primer ejemplo conocido de los de su clase. Las estancias de palacio son tan amplias y diáfanas que no resultan sobrecargadas aunque están ornamentadas con detalles de nada más y nada menos que seiscientos años de historia familiar y política: el antiquísimo escudo de armas, una abigarrada cámara de armaduras —cuya parte superior data del siglo XVI y la inferior del XV—, y las sedas de las paredes, que parecen querer aludir a las actividades comerciales de los Capponi en el pasado. La pieza más importante de la capilla privada —una pintura de Jacopo Pontormo titulada *La Madonna Capponi*—, está situada frente a la puerta de entrada. La luz se filtra en la nave a través de las vidrieras de cristal realizadas en 1526 por Guillaume de Marcillat. Otras obras del mismo pintor y una copia del ventanal adornan asimismo la renombrada capilla Capponi de la florentina iglesia de *Santa Felicita*. El palacio ha desempeñado incluso un papel en la moderna cinematografía como lugar de residencia y trabajo del personaje de ficción Hannibal Lecter en la película *Hannibal*. Y es que el conde Niccolò Capponi, profesor e historiador, ayudó a Thomas Harris a documentarse para escribir el libro ambientado en Florencia.

The Red Salon with painting of Niccolò Capponi's grandmother, born 1904, and the study.

Salone Rosso, con dipinti della nonna di Niccolò Capponi, nata nel 1904, e lo studio.

Der Rote Salon mit Gemälde von Niccolò Capponis Großmutter, die 1904 geboren wurde, sowie das Arbeitszimmer.

Le Salon rouge avec un tableau de la grand-mère de Niccolò Capponi, née en 1904, et le cabinet de travail.

Salón rojo con una pintura de la abuela de Niccolò Capponi, nacida en 1904, y estudio.

Entrance to the palace: *Niccolò Capponi, Alvaro (doorman) and Tanai (the palace cat). Porfido lion from an ancient Roman bath complex and Renaissance courtyard.*

L'entrata del palazzo: *Niccolò Capponi, Alvaro il portinaio, e Tanai, il gatto del palazzo. Il cortile rinascimentale e un antico leone in porfido proveniente da un complesso termale romano.*

Eingang zum Palast: *Niccolò Capponi, Portier Alvaro und Tanai, die Palastkatze. Ein Porfido-Löwe aus einem antiken römischen Bad und der Renaissance-Innenhof.*

L'entrée du palais : *Niccolò Capponi, Alvaro le portier et Tanai le chat. Un lion antique en porphyre, provenant de termes romains, et la cour Renaissance.*

Recibidor de palacio: *Niccolò Capponi, Alvaro el portero y Tanai el gato palaciego. Antiguo león de pórfido proveniente de unas termas romanas y patio renacentista.*

Lotteringhi della Stufa

Castello del Calcione, Lucignano

Originally the home of the monks of Saint Eugenius, the Castle of Calcione dates to the 11th century. A member of the powerful Campofregoso family held it until 1483, when political disagreements stripped him of his land and possessions. In that same year, the castle came into the current family's possession, when Luigi Lotteringhi della Stufa purchased it at auction. The family enjoyed good relations with the reigning Medici family for generations. Ancestor Agnolo Lotteringhi della Stufa was the friend of and ambassador to Sigismondo Malatesta, Lord of Rimini, a daring military leader and very good friend of Lorenzo de' Medici. In the 17th century, Fernando de' Medici bestowed the title of Marquis to the family.

Il Castello del Calcione, in origine dimora dei monaci di Sant'Eugenio, risale all'XI secolo. Rimase proprietà di un membro del potente casato dei Campofregoso fino al 1483, quando, in seguito a contese politiche, il nobile venne spogliato di terre e possedimenti. Quello stesso anno il castello passò alla famiglia che ancor oggi lo possiede, dopo che Luigi Lotteringhi della Stufa lo ebbe comprato all'asta. I membri del casato intrattennero per generazioni ottimi rapporti con i Medici. Uno degli antenati della famiglia, Agnolo Lotteringhi della Stufa, ambasciatore presso il signore di Rimini Sigismondo Malatesta, fu anche un valoroso combattente e buon amico di Lorenzo de' Medici. Nel XVII secolo Fernando de' Medici insignì la famiglia del titolo di marchesi.

Das Schloss von Calcione, das ursprünglich die Mönche des Heiligen Eugenius beherbergte, stammt aus dem 11. Jahrhundert. Bis ins Jahr 1483 gehörte es einem Familienmitglied des mächtigen Geschlechts der Campofregoso. Aufgrund politischer Auseinandersetzungen war dieser dann aber gezwungen, seinen Besitz aufzugeben. Im gleichen Jahr wurde das Schloss von der Familie, den heutigen Eigentümern, erworben, als Luigi Lotteringhi della Stufa es auf einer Auktion ersteigerte. Die Familie unterhielt bereits seit vielen Generationen gute Beziehungen zu den herrschenden Medici. Einer ihrer Vorfahren, Agnolo Lotteringhi della Stufa, war ein guter Freund und der Botschafter Sigismondo Malatestas, dem Herrn von Rimini, einem kühnen Condottiere und engen Vertrauten Lorenzo de' Medicis. Im 17. Jahrhundert erhob Fernando de' Medici die Familie in den Adelsstand und machte sie zu Markgrafen.

Ancien monastère où vivait une communauté fondée par saint Eugène, le château de Calcione date du XIe siècle. Un membre de la puissante famille des Campofregoso le détint jusqu'en 1483, date à laquelle des conflits politiques le privèrent de ses terres et autres possessions. La même année, il passa à la famille des propriétaires actuels, Luigi Lotteringhi della Stufa en ayant fait l'acquisition à une vente aux enchères. Pendant des générations, la famille eut de bons rapports avec ses souverains, les Médicis. Agnolo Lotteringhi della Stufa fut l'ami et l'ambassadeur de Sigismondo Malatesta, seigneur de Rimini, condottiere fougueux et proche de Laurent de Médicis. Au XVIIe siècle, Fernand de Médicis accorda le titre de marquis à la famille.

El castillo de Calcione, que en un principio fue el hogar de los monjes de la orden de san Eugenio, data del siglo XI. Estuvo en manos de un miembro de la poderosa familia Campofregoso hasta 1483, año en el que a causa de unas desavenencias políticas lo privaron de sus tierras y propiedades. Ese mismo año, el castillo pasó a ser propiedad de la familia que lo disfruta en la actualidad, al adquirirlo Luigi Lotteringhi della Stufa en una subasta. El clan gozó de buenas relaciones con la poderosa dinastía de los Médicis durante generaciones. Uno de los antepasados del linaje, Agnolo Lotteringhi della Stufa, fue amigo y embajador de Sigismondo Malatesta, señor de Rimini, un audaz jefe militar y estrecho amigo de Lorenzo de Médicis. En el siglo XVII, Fernando de Médicis otorgó el título del marquesado a la familia.

The Lotteringhi della Stufa coat of arms: the use of the traditional Florentine cross (between the lions) was granted to the family by the Republic of Florence.

La croce fra i leoni nello stemma dei Lotteringhi della Stufa rappresenta la croce del popolo fiorentino, donata alla famiglia dalla Repubblica.

Das Kreuz auf dem Familienwappen der Lotteringhi wurde der Familie von der Republik Florenz verliehen.

La croix figurant sur les armes des Lotteringhi della S... la République accorda à la famille pour son usage.

La cruz del escudo de armas de los Lotteringhi della Si... cuyo uso fue cedido a la familia por la República.

Sitting room with guns and *Sylvicapra Eritrea trophy.*

Salotto con armi e *trofeo di Sylvicapra Eritrea.*

Salon mit Waffen und einer *Trophäe einer Sylvicapra Eritrea.*

Salon avec armes à feu et trophée de Sylvicapra Eritrea.

Salón con armas y trofeo de caza de una Sylvicapra Eritrea.

The family has thrived at Castello del Calcione for generations, and shows a talent for uncovering Tuscan gastronomic secrets. In the 1930s a wall close to the cellar was removed during renovations. Discovered behind it were two ancient barriques, or barrels that had held *Vin Santo* (an Italian sweet wine), probably dating back to the 15th century. The wine, long since turned to vinegar, is now used as the base, or "mother," for making the estate's vinegar. In the 1960s, Maria Luisa Incontri Lotteringhi della Stufa (mother of current owner Bernardo) wrote two renowned books on Tuscany's history of food, including historic recipes. Her first book, *Desinari e Cene*, which won the grand prize for gastronomic literature in France in 1967, spans the time of the ancient Etruscans to the end of the 1400s. Her sequel book (1500 to modern times) is *Pranzi e Conviti*. The family continues the estate's food tradition by eating the organic food grown on the estate and making its own bread.

I Lotteringhi della Stufa hanno prosperato tra le mura del Castello del Calcione per molte generazioni, dimostrando un talento innato per la riscoperta dei segreti culinari della Toscana. Negli anni 1930, in seguito all'abbattimento di un muro confinante con la cantina nel corso di alcuni restauri, vennero alla luce due antiche barriques (botti) piene di vinsanto e forse risalenti al XV secolo. Quel vino, che si era ormai da tempo trasformato in aceto, viene oggi usato come base, o "matrice", per l'aceto prodotto nella tenuta. Negli anni 1960 Maria Luisa Incontri Lotteringhi della Stufa (madre dell'attuale proprietario, Bernardo) scrisse due famosi libri dedicati ai fasti della cucina Toscana e ricchi di ricette storiche. Il primo dei due, *Desinari e Cene*, vinse nel 1967 il premio per la letteratura gastronomica in Francia ed è dedicato al periodo che va dagli antichi etruschi alla fine del XV secolo. Il secondo (che copre i rimanenti anni, dal 1500 all'epoca moderna) è invece intitolato *Pranzi e Conviti*. La famiglia rende onore alla tradizione culinaria della tenuta nutrendosi del pane e dei cibi naturali ivi prodotti.

Die Familie lebt seit vielen Generationen auf dem Castello del Calcione und ist heute vor allem bekannt für das Lüften kulinarischer Geheimnisse der toskanischen Küche. Während Renovierungsarbeiten wurde in den Dreißiger Jahren des 20. Jahrhunderts im Keller eine Wand entfernt und dahinter zwei uralte Fässer entdeckt, die *Vin Santo* (einen italienischen Dessertwein) enthielten, der wahrscheinlich noch aus dem 15. Jahrhundert stammte. Der Wein, der schon lange zu Essig geworden war, wird nun als Basis oder Essigmutter für den Essig des Hauses verwendet. In den 1960er-Jahren schrieb Maria Luisa Incontri Lotteringhi della Stufa (die Mutter des heutigen Besitzers Bernardo) zwei erfolgreiche Bücher über die Geschichte des Essens in der Toskana, einschließlich historischer Rezepte. Ihr erstes Buch *Desinari e Cene*, das 1967 mit dem Großen Preis für gastronomische Literatur in Frankreich ausgezeichnet wurde, behandelt die Zeitspanne von den alten Etruskern bis zum Ende des 15. Jahrhunderts. Der zweite Band (von 1500 bis in die Moderne) trägt den Titel *Pranzi e Conviti*. Die Familie setzt auch heute noch diese traditionelle Zubereitung der Speisen fort, indem sie biologisch hergestellte Zutaten vom eigenen Gut verwendet und selbst ihr Brot backt.

Celle-ci, qui prospère à Castello del Calcione depuis des générations, possède le talent de révéler les secrets gastronomiques de la Toscane. Dans les années 1930, lors de rénovations, on démolit un mur près de la cave. On découvrit derrière deux barriques anciennes, remplies de *vin santo* (un vin doux italien), qui remontaient sans doute au XVe. Le vin, depuis longtemps aigri, sert désormais de « mère » pour l'élaboration du vinaigre de la propriété. Dans les années 1960, Maria Luisa Incontri Lotteringhi della Stufa (mère du propriétaire actuel, Bernardo) écrit deux livres célèbres sur l'histoire gastronomique de la Toscane, avec des recettes anciennes. Le premier, *Desinari e Cene*, qui remporta le grand prix de la littérature gastronomique en France en 1967, va de l'époque étrusque à la fin du XVe. Le second (de 1500 à l'époque contemporaine) a pour titre *Pranzi e Conviti*. La famille perpétue cette tradition gastronomique en consommant les aliments bio issus de la propriété et en faisant elle-même son pain.

El clan se ha multiplicado en el Castello del Calcione durante generaciones y en la actualidad muestra talento para revelar los secretos gastronómicos de la Toscana. En la década de 1930, se derribó una pared cercana a la bodega durante unos trabajos de remodelación. Tras el muro se descubrieron dos antiquísimas barricas que contenían un vino dulce italiano llamado *vin santo* probablemente del siglo XV. Este vino avinagrado por el paso del tiempo es el que se utiliza ahora como base o "madre" para hacer el vinagre de la estancia. En la década de 1960, Maria Luisa Incontri Lotteringhi della Stufa (madre de Bernardo, el actual propietario), escribió dos conocidos libros sobre la historia gastronómica de la Toscana, que incluían recetas antiguas. El primer volumen, titulado *Desinari e Cene*, que ganó el Gran Premio de Literatura Gastronómica de Francia en 1967, abarca un período de tiempo entre la época de los antiguos etruscos y el siglo XV. El segundo (que comprende los años entre 1500 a la actualidad) se titula *Pranzi e Conviti*. La familia continúa la tradición culinaria de la finca consumiendo los productos orgánicos de producción propia y haciendo incluso pan casero.

Letters, documents and a collection of footwarmers in the residence of Nicoletta and Bernardo Pianetti Lotteringhi della Stufa.

La casa di Nicoletta and Bernardo Pianetti Lotteringhi della Stufa con lettere, documenti e una collezione di scaldapiedi.

Briefe, Dokumente und eine Sammlung Fußwärmer im Hause von Nicoletta und Bernardo Pianetti Lotteringhi della Stufa.

Lettres, documents et une collection de chauffe-pieds chez Nicoletta et Bernardo Pianetti Lotteringhi della Stufa.

Cartas, documentos y una colección de calentadores para los pies en casa de Nicoletta y Bernardo Pianetti Lotteringhi della Stufa.

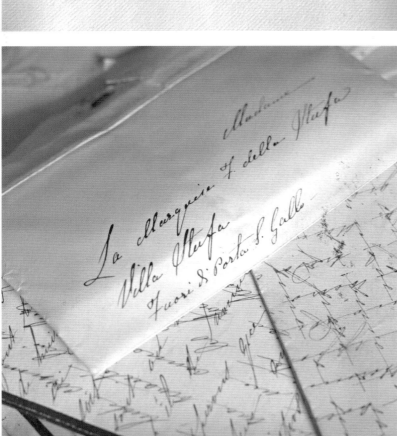

Two views of the main entrance: one with a cabreo (map) dating from 1808, the other with a coat of arms by Andrea della Robbia.

Due vedute dell'entrata principale, una con cabreo (mappa) del 1808, l'altra con lo stemma della famiglia, opera di Andrea della Robbia.

Zwei Ansichten des Haupteingangs — einmal mit einer Cabreo (Landkarte) aus dem Jahr 1808 und einmal mit dem Wappen von Andrea della Robbia.

Deux vues de l'entrée principale : l'une avec un cabreo (carte) de 1808, l'autre avec des armoiries réalisées par Andrea della Robbia.

Dos vistas de la entrada principal: una con un cabreo (mapa) de 1808, la otra con un escudo de armas de Andrea della Robbia.

Guicciardini Strozzi

Villa di Cusona, San Gimignano

Facing San Gimignano, famous for its towers, stands Villa di Cusona. The villa, which dates to 994, is the residence of the Guicciardini Strozzi family. Francesco Guicciardini was a statesman, (a contemporary of Machiavelli, who started his career as Guicciardini's secretary), Governor of the Papal States, philosopher and historian, and is possibly most known for his *Storia d'Italia*, detailing Italy's history from 1494 to 1532. The Strozzi men—powerful bankers, statesmen, successful merchants and commanders—were notorious rivals of the Medici. They were exiled from Florence in 1434 after Cosimo de' Medici gained power; the letters that Alessandra Macinghi Strozzi wrote during the exile have illuminated the lives of Renaissance women for historians and social scientists. The Strozzis thrived abroad in exile; on his return to Florence, Filippo Strozzi constructed Palazzo Strozzi. Piero Strozzi was Marshal of France, Commander in Chief of French Armed Forces; his bust stands testament to his service in the Gallery of the Battles in the Palace of Versailles.

Villa di Cusona sorge a San Gimignano, famosa per le sue torri. La villa, che risale al 994, è la residenza della famiglia Guicciardini Strozzi. Francesco Guicciardini fu uomo politico (nonché contemporaneo di Machiavelli, che cominciò la carriera proprio come suo segretario), governatore di alcune province dello stato della chiesa, filosofo e storico, forse meglio conosciuto per la sua *Storia d'Italia*, cronaca dettagliata delle vicende del paese dal 1494 a 1532. Gli uomini della famiglia Strozzi (potenti banchieri, politici, mercanti di successo e condottieri) erano antichi nemici della famiglia Medici, tanto che vennero banditi da Firenze nel 1434, in seguito alla salita al potere di Cosimo de' Medici. Le lettere che Alessandra Macinghi Strozzi scrisse dall'esilio sono documenti di grande valore storico e sociale che hanno permesso di ricostruire le abitudini delle nobildonne del rinascimento. Il casato, pur se in esilio, continuò comunque a prosperare tanto che, al suo rientro a Firenze, Filippo Strozzi fece subito iniziare i lavori per la costruzione di Palazzo Strozzi. Piero Strozzi divenne invece Maresciallo di Francia e servì nell'esercito francese in qualità di comandante; il busto in suo onore che ne commemora le imprese è conservato nella Galleria delle Battaglie della reggia di Versailles.

Gegenüber von San Gimignano, das für seine Geschlechtertürme berühmt ist, liegt die Villa di Cusona. Das Anwesen, dessen Ursprünge bis ins Jahr 994 zurückreichen, ist der Sitz der Familie Guicciardini Strozzi. Francesco Guicciardini war ein Staatsmann (ein Zeitgenosse Machiavellis, welcher seine berufliche Laufbahn als Guicciardinis Sekretär begann), päpstlicher Generalleutnant, Philosoph und Historiker. Vor allem ist er für seine *Storia d'Italia* bekannt, ein Werk, das sich mit der Geschichte Italiens von 1494 bis 1532 beschäftigt. Die Strozzi – mächtige Bankiers, Staatsmänner, einflussreiche Kaufleute und Feldherren – waren die berühmten Rivalen der Medici. Sie wurden 1434 nach der Machtübernahme Cosimo de' Medicis aus Florenz verbannt. Die Briefe, die Alessandra Macinghi Strozzi während ihres Exils verfasste, bieten Historikern und Soziologen einen interessanten Einblick in das Leben adeliger Frauen zur Zeit der Renaissance. Das Geschlecht der Strozzi blühte auch in der Verbannung weiter. Als Filippo Strozzi schließlich nach Florenz zurückkehrte, ließ er dort sogleich den Palazzo Strozzi erbauen. Piero Strozzi wiederum war Marschall von Frankreich und somit Befehlshaber der Französischen Armee. Aufgrund seiner Verdienste kann seine Büste in der Schlachtengalerie von Schloss Versailles bewundert werden.

Face à San Gimignano et à ses célèbres tours se dresse la Villa di Cusona, résidence des Guicciardini Strozzi et qui remonte à 994. Francesco Guicciardini fut un homme d'État (et un contemporain de Machiavel, qui débuta chez lui en qualité de secrétaire), gouverneur des États du pape, un philosophe et un historien, mais il est sans doute plus connu pour sa *Storia d'Italia*, qui détaille l'histoire de l'Italie de 1494 à 1532. Chez les Strozzi, les hommes – puissants banquiers, hommes d'État, négociants richissimes et chefs militaires – étaient les rivaux affichés des Médicis. Ils furent exilés de Florence en 1434, après l'accession au pouvoir de Côme de Médicis. Les lettres qu'écrivit Alessandra Macinghi Strozzi durant son exil jettent un jour sur la vie des femmes de la Renaissance pour les historiens et les chercheurs en sciences humaines. L'exil n'empêcha pas les Strozzi de s'enrichir et, une fois de retour à Florence, Filippo Strozzi fit élever le palais Strozzi. Piero Strozzi fut maréchal de France et son buste témoigne des services rendus dans la galerie des Batailles, à Versailles.

Situada frente a la localidad de San Gimignano, famosa por sus torres, se encuentra Villa di Cusona. Esta construcción, que data del año 994, es la residencia de la familia Guicciardini Strozzi. Francesco Guicciardini (un estadista contemporáneo de Maquiavelo, quien inició su carrera como su secretario), fue gobernador de los estados pontificios, filósofo e historiador. Probablemente su obra más conocida sea *Storia d'Italia*, un detallado tratado que recoge los avatares históricos de Italia entre 1494 y 1532. Los Strozzi, poderosos banqueros, destacados políticos y prósperos comerciantes y estrategas constituyeron notorios rivales de los Médicis. Fueron desterrados de Florencia en 1434 después de que Cosme de Médicis se hiciera con el poder. Las cartas que Alessandra Macinghi Strozzi escribiera desde el exilio constituyen un valioso testimonio de la vida de las mujeres renacentistas para historiadores y estudiosos sociales. Pero el clan prosperó y a su regreso a Florencia, Filippo Strozzi construyó el palacio del mismo nombre. Por su parte, Piero Strozzi llegó a ser mariscal de Francia, comandante en jefe de las fuerzas armadas galas. Su busto da fe de ello en la Galería de las Batallas del palacio de Versalles.

Details of Cusona's *magnificent gardens: a vista between rows of cypress; clipped boxwood and orci (terra cotta pots formerly used to store olive oil); and busts near the labyrinth.*

Particolari degli splendidi *giardini di Cusona: scorcio fra filari di cipressi, siepi di bosso e orci di terracotta un tempo usati per conservare l'olio d'oliva e busti scultorei nei pressi del labirinto.*

Detailansichten aus den *herrlichen Gärten von Cusona: Sichtachse einer Zypressenallee, Buchshecken und Orci – Terracottagefäße, in denen früher Olivenöl aufbewahrt wurde; sowie Büsten in der Nähe des Irrgartens.*

Détails des splendides *jardins de Cusona : vista entre deux rangées de cyprès; topiaires et orci, pots en terre cuite autrefois utilisés pour conserver l'huile d'olive ; et bustes près du labyrinthe.*

Detalles de los *magníficos jardines de Cusona: una vista entre las hileras de cipreses, boj podado y orci o vasijas de terracota para guardar aceite de oliva; busto junto al laberinto.*

Photographs, ballet shoes, and a Russian box are souvenirs from daughter Natalia's dance career. Daughter Irina plays the piano. Livery buttons and fabric with the Strozzi coat of arms.

Fotografie, scarpe da punta e carillon, souvenir della carriera di ballerina della figlia Natalia. La figlia Irina suona il piano. Tessuti e bottoni da livrea con lo stemma degli Strozzi.

Fotografien, Ballettschuhe und eine russische Dose sind Erinnerungsstücke an die Ballettzeit der Tochter Natalia. Tochter Irina spielt Klavier. Livreeknöpfe und Stoff mit dem Familienwappen der Strozzi.

Quelques photographies, des chaussons de pointes et des poupées russes évoquent la carrière de danseuse de Natalia. Sa sœur Irina joue du piano. Boutons de livrée et tissu arborant les armes des Strozzi.

Fotografías, zapatillas de ballet y una caja rusa son algunos de los recuerdos de la dedicación a la danza de una de las hijas, Natalia. La otra, Irina, toca el piano. Botones de librea y paño con el escudo de armas de los Strozzi.

The Guicciardini Strozzi family looks to the Cusona Estate for both relaxation and work. An ornate music room hints of elegant entertainment, and photographs and souvenirs of the ballet give a glimpse of the talented family. In addition, the family continues the estate's generations of careful agriculture, and particularly, its production of wines. Prince Girolamo Strozzi's grandfather, Francesco Guicciardini, who was Minister of Agriculture and Foreign Affairs from 1906 to 1909, as well as Mayor of Florence, transformed Cusona into an innovative and model estate. Today, the family continues and enhances Cusona's time-honored winemaking tradition through modern methods and the development of new wines.

La famiglia Guicciardini Strozzi continua a vivere e lavorare a Villa di Cusona. Al suo interno una sala per la musica riccamente decorata rievoca un passato di spettacoli ed eleganza, mentre le foto e i trofei del balletto accennano al talento di famiglia. I Guicciardini Strozzi, ormai da generazioni, tramandano la tradizione agricola del casato, in particolare la produzione del vino. Francesco Guicciardini, nonno del principe Girolamo Strozzi, fu ministro dell'agricoltura e degli esteri dal 1906 al 1909, nonché sindaco di Firenze, e trasformò la Cusona in un perfetto esempio di villa moderna. Oggi la famiglia continua l'antica tradizione vinicola arricchendone il prestigio grazie all'uso delle tecnologie più avanzate e allo sviluppo di vini sempre nuovi.

Die Familie Guicciardini Strozzi betrachtet das Landgut Cusona sowohl als einen Ort der Entspannung als auch der Arbeit. Das reich verzierte Musikzimmer weist auf eine lange Kultur unterhaltsamer Zusammenkünfte hin und die zahlreichen Fotografien und Gegenstände zum Ballett sind Zeugnis des künstlerischen Talents dieser Familie. Die Guicciardini Strozzi führen seit vielen Generationen die Landwirtschaft des Anwesens, was sich vor allem in der Weinproduktion niederschlägt. Der Großvater des Prinzen Girolamo Strozzi, Francesco Guicciardini, war von 1906 bis 1909 italienischer Landwirtschafts- und Außenminister und Bürgermeister von Florenz und verwandelte Cusona in ein innovatives und vorbildlich geführtes Gut. Heutzutage setzt die Familie die seit langer Zeit hochgeschätzte Tradition der Weinproduktion mit modernen Mitteln fort und hat zahlreiche neue Weine entwickelt.

La famille Guicciardini Strozzi considère la Villa di Cusona comme un lieu de détente et de travail. La salle de musique raffinée évoque des distractions élégantes, tandis que les photographies et les souvenirs de ballets donnent une idée des talents de cette famille. En outre, elle perpétue sur ses terres la tradition agricole et, en particulier, la production vinicole. Le grand-père du prince Girolamo Strozzi, Francesco Guicciardini, qui fut ministre de l'Agriculture et des Affaires étrangères de 1906 à 1909, ainsi que maire de Florence, transforma Cusona en un domaine innovant et exemplaire. Aujourd'hui, la famille perpétue et améliore la longue tradition viticole de Cusona, grâce à des méthodes de pointe et à l'élaboration de nouveaux vins.

La familia Guicciardini Strozzi se sirve de Villa di Cusona tanto para descansar como para trabajar. Una recargada sala de música es prueba de su gusto por los entretenimientos refinados, y la colección de fotografías y *souvenirs de ballet* da una idea del talento familiar. Además, las nuevas generaciones del clan continúan con la tradición agrícola, en especial con la producción de vinos. Francesco Guicciardini, abuelo del príncipe Girolamo Strozzi, que fue ministro de agricultura y asuntos exteriores de 1906 a 1909 y también alcalde de Florencia, transformó Villa Cusona en una hacienda ejemplar e innovadora. Actualmente, la familia continúa mejorando la antigua tradición de Cusona, haciendo honor a la explotación vitivinícola por medio del uso métodos modernos y la creación de nuevos vinos.

Previous page: Girolamo and Irina Guicciardini Strozzi with their two daughters, Irina and Natalia.

Pagina precedente: Girolamo e Irina Guicciardini Strozzi con le figlie Irina e Natalia.

Vorherige Seite: Girolamo und Irina Guicciardini Strozzi mit den Töchtern Irina und Natalia.

Page précédent : Girolamo et Irina Guicciardini Strozzi, avec leurs deux filles, Irina et Natalia.

Página anterior: Girolamo e Irina Guicciardini Stozzi con sus dos hijas, Irina y Natalia.

Girolamo's library with family tree dating back to the 1700s. The fireplace in the sitting room bears the Guicciardini coat of arms.

Lo studio di Girolamo, con l'albero genealogico della famiglia dal XVIII secolo. Il camino del salotto reca lo stemma dei Guicciardini.

Die Bibliothek von Girolamo Guicciardini Strozzi mit einem Stammbaum aus dem 18. Jahrhundert. Am Kamin im Salon ist das Familienwappen der Guicciardini zu sehen.

La bibliothèque de Girolamo, avec l'arbre généalogique de la famille, qui remonte au XVIIIe siècle. La cheminée du salon est ornée des armes des Guicciardini.

Biblioteca de Girolamo, con árbol genealógico del siglo XVIII. Sobre la chimenea de la sala, el escudo de armas de Guicciardini.

Pandolfini

Villa di Tizzano, Antella

The family Pandolfini appears repeatedly in the history of Florence, with several family members devoting their lives in service to the Church, including Cardinal Niccolò Pandolfini (1440–1518) and Bishop Giannozzo Pandolfini; other family members served in civic affairs including: Agnolo Pandolfini (1361–1446), a statesman, whose essay *Del governo della famiglia* illuminates the home life of the nobleman in the Renaissance; and Pierfilippo Pandolfini was Cosimo de'Medici's ambassador to Venice. Pandolfino da Rinucciano, the founder of the family became a notary, and was followed in this profession by many generations of his descendants. It proved to be a shrewd choice as Florence was a very wealthy merchant town with frequent real estate dealings needing notarization. The family is particularly noted for its patronage of the arts over generations, and its ties to the arts continue today. Elisabetta Pandolfini is a sculptress, and enlivens her home, Villa di Tizzano with many of her pieces.

Quello della famiglia Pandolfini è un nome ricorrente nelle cronache della città di Firenze. Vari membri del casato dedicarono la propria vita al servizio della Chiesa, come il cardinale Niccolò Pandolfini (1440–1518) o il vescovo Giannozzo Pandolfini, mentre altri si distinsero per il loro ruolo politico, come Agnolo Pandolfini (1361–1446), statista (che nel trattato *Del governo della famiglia* descrive usi e costumi familiari dei nobiluomini del Rinascimento), o Pierfilippo Pandolfini, che fu ambasciatore a Venezia per conto di Cosimo de' Medici. Il capostipite della famiglia, Pandolfino da Rinucciano, scelse la professione notarile e molti suoi discendenti, per varie generazioni, ne seguirono l'esempio. La sua fu una scelta accorta e felice, poiché Firenze era una ricchissima città mercantile in cui le transazioni riguardanti gli immobili, richiedenti la certificazione di un notaio, erano numerosissime. La famiglia è nota in particolare per il patrocinio delle arti, tradizione che non è mai venuta meno fino ai giorni nostri. Elisabetta Pandolfini è una scultrice ed ha arricchito la Villa di Tizzano, dove abita, con numerose delle sue opere.

Die Familie Pandolfini spielte in der Geschichte der Stadt Florenz immer wieder eine wichtige Rolle. Mehrere Familienmitglieder stellten ihr Leben in den Dienst der Kirche, wie zum Beispiel der Kardinal Niccolò Pandolfini (1440–1518) oder der Bischof Giannozzo Pandolfini. Andere waren Staatsdiener – wie der Staatsmann Agnolo Pandolfini (1361–1446), dessen Essay *Del governo della famiglia* das Familienleben eines Adeligen der Renaissance lebendig werden lässt, oder Pierfilippo Pandolfini, der Gesandter Cosimo de' Medicis in Venedig war. Pandolfino da Rinucciano, der Gründer des Geschlechts, war Notar – ein Beruf, der auch von vielen seiner unzähligen Nachfahren ergriffen wurde. Eine gute Wahl, wie sich herausstellte, denn Florenz war eine äußerst florierende Handelsstadt mit häufig wechselnden Liegenschaften, wozu stets ein Notar benötigt wurde. Die Familie Pandolfini ist vor allem für ihr Mäzenatentum berühmt, das sie über viele Generationen hinweg pflegte, und diese enge Verbindung zur Kunst hat auch heute noch Bestand. Elisabetta Pandolfini arbeitet als Bildhauerin und belebt ihr Heim, die Villa di Tizzano, mit zahlreichen eigenen Arbeiten.

La famille Pandolfini apparaît à maintes reprises dans l'histoire de Florence, plusieurs de ses membres ayant consacré leur vie au service de l'Église, tels le cardinal Niccolò Pandolfini (1440–1518) et l'évêque Giannozzo Pandolfini. Certains choisirent de servir leur patrie, notamment Agnolo Pandolfini (1361–1446), un homme d'État dont l'essai *Del governo della famiglia* révèle la vie familiale du noble italien de la Renaissance, et Pierfilippo Pandolfini, qui fut ambassadeur de Côme de Médicis à Venise. Pandolfino da Rinucciano, le fondateur de la famille, devint notaire, profession qu'embrassèrent après lui plusieurs générations de ses descendants. Ce qui se révéla un choix astucieux, Florence étant une ville commerçante très riche, où les biens immobiliers changeaient fréquemment de mains – et nécessitaient des actes notariés. La famille, qui s'est distinguée par son mécénat depuis des siècles, a maintenu ses liens avec le monde artistique. Elisabetta Pandolfini sculpte et a orné sa demeure, la Villa di Tizzano, de nombre de ses œuvres.

La familia Pandolfini aparece citada repetidamente en la historia de Florencia. Muchos miembros del clan pusieron su vida al servicio de la Iglesia, entre ellos, el cardenal Niccolò Pandolfini (1440–1518) y el obispo Giannozzo Pandolfini; otros se dedicaron a asuntos más mundanos, por ejemplo, Agnolo Pandolfini (1361–1446), un estadista cuyo ensayo *Del governo della famiglia* arroja luz sobre la vida hogareña de los nobles durante el Renacimiento; también destaca Pierfilippo Pandolfini, embajador en Venecia de Cosme de Médicis. Pandolfino da Rinucciano, el fundador de la dinastía, se hizo notario, y en el ejercicio de esa profesión le siguieron sus descendientes durante varias generaciones. Está claro que fue una astuta decisión, porque Florencia era una próspera ciudad mercantil con infinidad de negocios inmobiliarios que debían registrarse notarialmente. Además la familia ha destacado muy especialmente en el mecenazgo de las artes durante generaciones y sus vínculos con este mundo perviven hasta nuestros días. La escultora Elisabetta Pandolfini alegra su hogar, Villa di Tizzano, con sus propias obras.

Elisabetta Pandolfini's artistic eye has matched colors and décor to enhance the Villa di Tizzano: the entry, 1930s bathroom and bedroom.

Lo sguardo d'artista di Elisabetta Pandolfini ha guidato la scelta di colori e decori per esaltare la bellezza di Villa di Tizzano: entrata, bagno e camera da letto degli anni Trenta.

Es ist Elisabetta Pandolfinis künstlerischem Geschick zu verdanken, dass die Villa di Tizzano stilistisch eine solche Einheit bildet: der Eingang, Badezimmer und Schlafzimmer aus den 1930er Jahren.

Avec son œil d'artiste, Elisabetta Pandolfini a su harmoniser les couleurs et le décor pour mettre en valeur la Villa di Tizzano : l'entrée, la salle de bain et la chambre des années 1930.

Elisabetta Pandolfini, con su sentido artístico, ha sabido conjuntar los colores y la decoración para realzar la belleza de Villa di Tizzano: recibidor, cuarto de baño y alcoba de los años 1930.

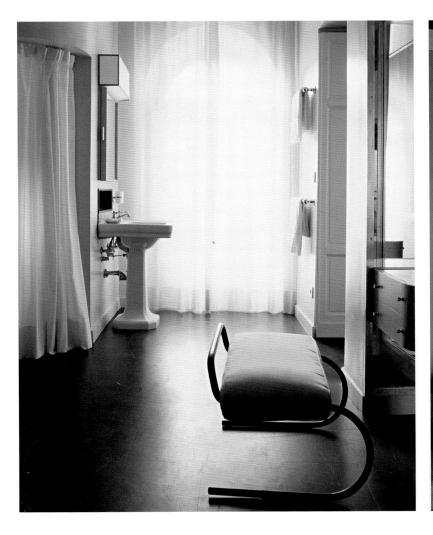

Elisabetta Pandolfini's sculptures "The Philosopher" and a tribute to Alberto Giacometti near an olive grove.

Le sculture di *Elisabetta Pandolfini "Il filosofo" e un tributo ad Alberto Giacometti nei pressi di un uliveto.*

Elisabetta Pandolfinis *Skulptur „Der Philosoph" und eine Hommage an Alberto Giacometti vor einem Olivenhain.*

Sculptures d'Elisabetta Pandolfini : *« Le Philosophe » et, près d'une oliveraie, un hommage à Alberto Giacometti.*

Las esculturas de *Elisabetta Pandolfini "El filósofo" y un tributo a Alberto Giacometti junto a un olivar.*

Next pages: *The villa's view over the infinity-edge pool includes Florence and the hills beyond.*

Pagina successiva: *Dal bordo a filo della piscina lo sguardo si spinge fino a Firenze e alle colline oltre la città.*

Nächste Seite: *Blick von der Villa über den randlosen Pool auf die Hügellandschaft in Richtung Florenz.*

Page suivante: *De la villa et par-delà la piscine à débordement, vue sur Florence et les collines environnantes.*

Página siguiente: *La vista de la villa sobre la piscina de borde infinito se abre hacia Florencia y las colinas del horizonte.*

With its panoramic view in the Chianti hills surrounding Florence, the location of Villa di Tizzano has proved to be highly desirable, and the property has been molded and shaped to meet the changing needs and whims of the ages since medieval times. Given its perspective of the surrounding countryside, it is not surprising the property is first documented as the location for 11th century observation tower. Then, in the 16th century, the building was expanded and adapted for family life, which was furthered in the 19th century. In more modern times, the parents of Elisabetta Pandolfini significantly restored the home, adding contemporary touches, such as the wood and glass entry that encloses the staircase to the second floor, and an elegant 1930s bathroom. They also engaged the highly sought-after English architect, Cecil Pinsent to design a two-acre garden that begins at the front yard of the house. Elisabetta has brought the villa to its highest level of charm and character; she engaged Alex Hamilton, the English designer, to help with the décor. The paint colors for each room are all natural colors, matched to 19th century natural pigments.

Villa di Tizzano, con la sua vista panoramica sulle colline del Chianti, vicino a Firenze, sorge in una posizione invidiabile, e fin dal medioevo la tenuta è stata continuamente ristrutturata e modellata per venire incontro ai gusti e ai capricci delle varie epoche. Data questa sua posizione di dominio sulla campagna circostante, non sorprende il fatto che nei primi documenti che la riguardano, risalenti al XI secolo, la proprietà sia indicata come torre di avvistamento. In seguito, nel XVI secolo, l'edificio venne ampliato e trasformato in abitazione civile, quindi ulteriormente ingrandito nel XIX secolo. In epoca più recente, i genitori di Elisabetta Pandolfini hanno compiuto ampi restauri sulla villa, aggiungendole tocchi di modernità come l'atrio in legno con vetrate che racchiude lo scalone che porta al secondo piano o un elegante bagno in stile anni 1930. Sempre grazie a loro, il ricercatissimo architetto inglese Cecil Pinsent è stato ingaggiato per progettare un giardino di quasi 8.000 m² che parte dalla corte anteriore della casa. Elisabetta ha portato la villa all'apice del suo splendore, donandole ancor più carattere e affidandone la decorazione ad Alex Hamilton, famoso designer inglese. Ogni stanza è stata dipinta con colori naturali che ricreano i pigmenti originali del XIX secolo.

Durch die herrliche Aussicht auf die hügelige Landschaft der Chianti-Region um Florenz besitzt die Villa di Tizzano eine außergewöhnliche Lage. Das Anwesen wurde seit dem Mittelalter über die Jahrhunderte hinweg immer wieder aus- und umgebaut, um den jeweiligen Wünschen und Anforderungen der Bewohner zu entsprechen. Betrachtet man den Ausblick auf die Umgebung, ist es nicht weiter verwunderlich, dass bereits im 11. Jahrhundert dort ein Wachturm entstand. Im 16. Jahrhundert wurde das Gebäude dann erweitert und so ausgebaut, dass die Familie einziehen konnte; bis zum 19. Jahrhundert fanden immer wieder bauliche Veränderungen statt. Im 20. Jahrhundert ließen Elisabetta Pandolfinis Eltern die Villa von Grund auf restaurieren und fügten zugleich einige moderne Umbauten hinzu – wie zum Beispiel die Eingangshalle aus Glas und Holz, von wo aus die Treppe in den ersten Stock führt, sowie ein elegantes Badezimmer im Stil der Dreißiger Jahre. Sie verpflichteten zudem den begehrten englischen Architekten Cecil Pinsent, einen 8.000 m² großen Garten zu entwerfen, der vor dem Haus angelegt ist. Elisabetta hat seitdem die Villa zu einem wahren Schmuckstück werden lassen. Für das Dekor beauftragte sie den englischen Designer Alex Hamilton, der für alle Räume natürliche Farben wählte, um sie mit den natürlichen Pigmenten aus dem 19. Jahrhundert anzugleichen.

Avec sa vue panoramique sur les collines du Chianti qui entourent Florence, la Villa di Tizzano jouit d'un emplacement des plus remarquables. Depuis le Moyen Âge, elle a subi de nombreux remaniements pour suivre l'évolution des besoins et des goûts. Étant donné la perspective qu'elle offre sur la campagne environnante, il n'y a rien de surprenant à ce que la propriété ait été mentionnée pour la première fois au XIe siècle comme tour d'observation. Le bâtiment fut agrandi et adapté à la vie de famille au XVIe, puis encore perfectionné au XIXe. À une époque plus récente, les parents d'Elisabetta Pandolfini ont procédé à des restaurations importantes et ajouté quelques touches contemporaines, telles que l'entrée en bois et en verre qui entoure la cage d'escalier jusqu'au deuxième étage, ou une élégante salle de bain style 1930. Ils engagèrent également un paysagiste anglais très recherché, Cecil Pinsent, qui dessina le parc de 8.000 m² entourant la demeure. Elisabetta, qui a porté la villa à son plus haut niveau de charme et de caractère, a fait appel à Alex Hamilton, le décorateur anglais. Les couleurs des peintures de chaque pièce sont toutes naturelles et assorties aux pigments naturels du XIXe.

Con su panorámica vista sobre las colinas de Chianti que rodean Florencia, el emplazamiento de Villa di Tiziano ha sido siempre muy apreciado. Desde el medievo, la propiedad ha sido remodelada y reestructurada en numerosas ocasiones para responder a las cambiantes necesidades y los caprichos de cada época. Teniendo en cuenta las vistas que se disfrutan desde esta finca sobre las tierras que la rodean, no es sorprendente que las primeras documentaciones que existen sobre ella ya en el siglo XI den fe de la existencia de una atalaya en su emplazamiento. Posteriormente en el siglo XVI, la construcción se amplió y se adaptó para convertirse en una residencia familiar. En esta forma pervivió hasta el siglo XIX. En tiempos más recientes, los padres de Elisabetta Pandolfini hicieron una completa remodelación de la casa y le añadieron toques modernos como la entrada de madera y cristal desde la que parte la escalera hasta el segundo piso, y un elegante cuarto de baño en estilo de los años treinta. Asimismo contrataron al renombrado arquitecto inglés Cecil Pinsent para diseñar el jardín de 8.000 m², que se extiende delante del edificio. Elisabetta ha logrado elevar la casa a su mayor nivel de encanto y carácter. Fue ella quien pidió al diseñador inglés Alex Hamilton que la asesorara con la decoración de la villa. Las pinturas en tonos naturales que recubren las paredes de todas las habitaciones emulan los pigmentos del siglo XIX.

Angelica Dalgas, daughter of Elisabetta Pandolfini, in the grand dining room—the villa's former ballroom.

Angelica Dalgas, figlia di Elisabetta Pandolfini, nella vasta sala da pranzo, un tempo sala da ballo.

Angelica Dalgas, Tochter von Elisabetta Pandolfini, im großen Speisezimmer, dem früheren Ballsaal der Villa.

Angelica Dalgas, fille d'Elisabetta Pandolfini, dans l'immense salle à manger — l'ancienne salle de bal de la villa.

Angelica Dalgas, hija de Elisabetta Pandolfini, en el espacioso comedor, antiguo salón de baile de la villa.

Cervini

Vivo d'Orcia, Castiglione d'Orcia

The closely-knit Cervini family owns Palazzo Cervini, on the slopes of Monte Amiata, above the Val d'Orcia near the town of Vivo d'Orcia (where the Vivo River invisibly springs to life). The palace's external austerity brings to mind this family's famous predecessor who purchased the estate in the 1530s, Cardinal Marcello Cervini. Marcello, who was known for his integrity, church reform, and austere personal habits, would become Pope Marcellus II on April 9, 1555. Though his Papal dominion would last a short 22 days, his life in the church was illustrious and storied. Cardinal Marcello served as secretary to Pope Paul III, and close advisor to the Pope's young nephew, Alessandro Farnese. He advanced scholarship during his leadership of the Vatican library, acquiring hundreds of Latin, Greek and Hebrew volumes, and causing ancient others to be printed. He represented the Pope as one of three Presidents of the Council of Trent, which attracted the wrath of Charles V, Holy Roman Emporer. His own papacy is honored in Palestrina's *Mass of Pope Marcellus*, which was composed posthumously.

Quella dei Cervini è una famiglia molto unita e possiede il palazzo omonimo collocato sulle pendici del Monte Amiata in Val d'Orcia, nei pressi di Vivo d'Orcia (dove il fiume Vivo sembra sgorgare dal nulla). L'austerità dell'esterno del palazzo rimanda a un famoso antenato della famiglia, il cardinale Marcello Cervini, responsabile dell'acquisto della tenuta attorno al 1530. Questo personaggio, famoso per la sua rettitudine, per le riforme ecclesiastiche e i modi estremamente severi, il 9 aprile 1555 diventò Papa con il nome di Marcello II. Anche se il suo pontificato durò solo 22 giorni, ebbe un'illustre e ricca vita ecclesiastica: quando era cardinale fu segretario di Papa Paolo III e consigliere personale del giovane nipote del pontefice, Alessandro Farnese; nel corso della sua direzione della Biblioteca Vaticana contribuì enormemente allo sviluppo del patrimonio culturale acquistando centinaia di volumi in latino, greco ed ebraico e facendo ristampare molti testi antichi; infine fu uno dei tre legati papali e Presidente in quel Concilio di Trento che tanto fece infuriare Carlo V, imperatore del Sacro Romano Impero. Alla sua morte il compositore Giovanni da Palestrina gli dedicò la *Missa Papae Marcelli*.

Der Palazzo Cervini befindet sich im Besitz der Familie Cervini, die sich durch einen engen Familienverbund auszeichnet, und steht am Hang des Monte Amiata über dem Val d'Orcia in der Nähe des Städtchens Vivo d'Orcia (wo der Vivo unsichtbar entspringt). In seiner äußeren Strenge erinnert der Palast an Kardinal Marcello Cervini – den berühmten Vorfahren, der in den Dreißigerjahren des 16. Jahrhunderts das Anwesen erwarb. Der Kirchenmann, der für seine Integrität, seine Reformbemühungen innerhalb der Kirche und äußerste Strenge gegen sich selbst bekannt war, wurde am 9. April 1555 zum Papst Marcellus II. gewählt. Sein Pontifikat dauerte zwar nur 22 Tage, doch sein Leben als Kirchenmann war dafür umso illustrer und glänzender. Kardinal Marcello diente als persönlicher Sekretär Papst Paul III. und fungierte als enger Berater für Alessandro Farnese, der ein Neffe des Papstes war. Während seiner Zeit als Kardinalsbibliothekar fügte er dem Bestand der vatikanischen Bibliothek Hunderte von lateinischen, griechischen und hebräischen Bänden hinzu und ließ andere alte Schriften drucken. Er vertrat den Papst als einer von drei Vorsitzenden beim Konzil von Trient, das den Zorn Kaiser Karls V. auf sich zog. Marcellos Pontifikat ist die *Messe für Papst Marcellus* gewidmet, die Palestrina nach dessen Tod komponierte.

Les Cervini, une famille très unie, sont les propriétaires du palais Cervini, qui est situé sur un versant du Monte Amiata, au-dessus du Val d'Orcia, près de la ville de Vivo d'Orcia où se trouvent les sources invisibles du Vivo. Les extérieurs austères du palais rappellent l'illustre ancêtre qui l'acheta dans les années 1530, le cardinal Marcello Cervini. Connu pour son intégrité, sa volonté de réforme religieuse et la sévérité de son mode de vie, il devint pape sous le nom de Marcel II le 9 avril 1555. Son pontificat ne dura que 22 jours, mais sa vie religieuse fut illustre et édifiante. Le cardinal Cervini avait été le secrétaire du pape Paul III et avait veillé à l'éducation de son jeune neveu, Alessandro Farnese. Directeur de la bibliothèque du Vatican, il acquit des centaines de volumes en latin, en grec et en hébreu et fit imprimer nombre de textes antiques. Lors du concile de Trente, il représenta le pape et fut l'un des trois prélats à présider, ce qui lui valut l'hostilité de Charles Quint, empereur du Saint Empire. Palestrina a immortalisé son pontificat par la *Messe du pape Marcel*, qui fut composée après sa mort.

La familia Cervini, unida por estrechos lazos, es la propietaria del palacio del mismo nombre, que situado en las faldas del monte Amiata preside el Val d'Orcia, no lejos de la localidad de Vivo d'Orcia (donde el río Vivo nace de forma imperceptible). El sobrio aspecto exterior del palacio nos recuerda a un famoso antepasado de esta familia, que compró la hacienda en la década de 1530: el cardenal Marcello Cervini. Marcello, conocido por su integridad, por la reforma eclesiástica en la que participó y por sus austeros hábitos personales, se convirtió en el papa Marcello II el 9 de abril de 1555. Aunque su mandato pontificio duró sólo veintidós días, su trayectoria eclesiástica fue ilustre e hizo historia. En su calidad de cardenal fue secretario del Papa Pablo III y consejero de confianza del joven sobrino del pontífice, Alessandro Farnese. Como director de la biblioteca vaticana, fomentó la erudición y la ciencia adquiriendo cientos de libros en latín, griego y hebreo, y encargando la impresión de volúmenes antiguos. Representó al Papa como uno de los tres presidentes del Concilio de Trento, que desató la ira de Carlos V, emperador del Santo Imperio Romano Germánico. Palestrina compuso post mórtem la *Misa del Papa Marcello* en honor a este pontífice.

The *palazzo's* Salotto Rosso (Red Salon) with cotto impruneta and marble floor from the beginning of the 1900s. The portrait is of Maria Elisabetta Cervini (née Galeotti).

Il Salotto Rosso del palazzo, con pavimento di marmo e cotto impruneta degli inizi del XX secolo. Il ritratto raffigura Maria Elisabetta Cervini (nata Galeotti).

Der Salotto Rosso (Rote Salon) mit Cotto Impruneta und Marmorboden aus dem frühen 20. Jahrhundert. Auf dem Porträt sieht man Maria Elisabetta Cervini (geborene Galeotti).

Le Salotto Rosso (Salon rouge) du palais, avec son sol en cotto impruneta et marbre, datant du début du XXᵉ siècle, et le portrait de Maria Elisabetta Cervini (née Galeotti).

Salotto Rosso (salón rojo) de palacio con cotto impruneta y suelos de mármol de principios del siglo XX. El retrato que decora la estancia es de Maria Elisabetta Cervini (nombre de soltera Galeotti).

The kitchen table stands close to the room-sized fireplace—an important source of heat in winter.

Il tavolo della cucina si trova accanto al gigantesco camino, ottima fonte di calore nei mesi invernali.

Der Küchentisch befindet sich in der Nähe des zimmergroßen Kamins – eine wichtige Wärmequelle während des Winters.

La table de la cuisine est située près de l'immense cheminée, une excellente source de chaleur en hiver.

La mesa de la cocina se encuentra junto a la enorme chimenea que constituye una buena fuente de calor en invierno.

Palazzo Cervini dates to near the year 1000, though its early life was as a monastery, devoted to the monks of Camaldoli. Saint Romualdo, the founder of the Camaldoli monks may have started the reclusive Order here in the 11th century. The palazzo served as a monastery until the 1500s; its kitchen dates to the monastery's later years. Eschewing the expressive and dramatic ornamentation of the day, Cardinal Marcello engaged Antonio da Sangallo the Younger to rebuild it, and reinvigorated the estate into an efficient agricultural enterprise during his years here. In the 19th century, the Cervini family added a spur to support the structure, as it had begun to succumb to gravity, and move down the hill. Though the structure remains epic in its external austerity, there are warm elements: the Italianate garden outside, and interiors warmed by immense fireplaces, and rooms that abound with the keepsakes and furnishings of centuries of Cervini family life.

Palazzo Cervini risale circa all'anno mille, anche se a quei tempi era un monastero dei monaci camaldolesi. San Romualdo, fondatore dell'ordine di Camaldoli, forse diede origine alla confraternita proprio tra le sue mura, nell'XI secolo. Il palazzo rimase un monastero fino al XVI secolo e la cucina risale ancora a quest'ultimo periodo. Il cardinale Marcello, contrario agli ornamenti eccessivi e vistosi tipici della sua epoca, ingaggiò Antonio da Sangallo il Giovane per ricostruire il palazzo, trasformando la tenuta, nel periodo in cui vi abitò, in una produttiva azienda agricola. Nel XIX secolo la famiglia Cervini fece aggiungere dei contrafforti per sostenere la struttura dell'edificio, che aveva cominciato a cedere sotto il suo peso, rischiando di rovinare a valle. Anche se esteriormente ha mantenuto intatta la sua imponente austerità, non è privo di elementi che ne addolciscono l'immagine: ne sono un esempio il giardino all'italiana, gli interni riscaldati dagli immensi camini o le sale colme di ricordi e arredi appartenuti ai Cervini di ogni epoca.

Der Palazzo Cervini wurde um das Jahr 1000 errichtet und war ursprünglich ein Kloster, das den Mönchen von Camaldoli gehörte. Der Heilige Romualdo, der Gründer der Camaldolis, rief hier möglicherweise selbst diesen zurückgezogen lebenden Orden im 11. Jahrhundert ins Leben. Bis ins 16. Jahrhundert diente das Gebäude als Kloster, die Küche stammt aus den letzten Jahren des Klosters. Kardinal Marcello, der die ausdrucksstarke und dramatische Ornamentierung seiner Zeit nicht mochte, beauftragte Antonio da Sangallo den Jüngeren mit dem Umbau. Auch schaffte er es, das dazugehörige Land durch eine effiziente Bewirtschaftung voll zu nutzen. Im 19. Jahrhundert fügten die Cervinis dem Palazzo eine zusätzliche Tragekonstruktion hinzu, da er drohte, der Schwerkraft nachzugeben und den Hang hinabzurutschen. Auch wenn der Gesamteindruck noch immer eher archaisch wirkt, gibt es durchaus warme Elemente: der italienische Garten vor dem Haus, die gewaltigen Kamine, welche die Räumlichkeiten wärmen, und auch die Zimmer sind voller Erinnerungsstücke und Möbel, die von einem jahrhundertelangen Familienleben der Cervinis zeugen.

Le palais Cervini construit aux alentours de l'an mil, était à l'origine un monastère où vivaient les moines de Camaldoli. C'est sans doute ici que saint Romualdo fonda la communauté des camaldules, au XIe siècle. L'édifice, qui servit de couvent jusqu'au XVIe, a conservé sa cuisine monacale. Rejetant l'ornementation expressive et dramatique alors en vogue, le cardinal Cervini engagea Antonio da Sangallo le Jeune pour le reconstruire et il transforma la propriété en une entreprise agricole performante. Au XIXe siècle, les Cervini firent bâtir un éperon pour soutenir la structure qui avait commencé à succomber à la gravité et à descendre la colline. Si le palais frappe toujours par son austérité extérieure, il comporte des éléments chaleureux : le parc à l'italienne et les intérieurs réchauffés par d'immenses cheminées ou les pièces où s'accumulent souvenirs et témoignages des siècles de vie familiale chez les Cervini.

El palacio Cervini data aproximadamente del año 1000, aunque originalmente fue un monasterio consagrado a los monjes de Camaldoli. Es posible que san Romualdo, fundador de la orden de clausura camaldulense, la instaurara precisamente en este lugar en el siglo XI. El palacio fue la sede de los religiosos hasta el siglo XVI; la cocina data de los últimos años del monasterio. Evitando la excesiva y dramática decoración propia del tiempo, el cardenal Marcello encargó la remodelación del edificio al arquitecto Antonio da Sangallo el Joven y convirtió la estancia en una productiva hacienda agrícola durante los años que pasó en ella. En el siglo XIX, la familia Cervini añadió un contrafuerte para sujetar la estructura que había empezado a sucumbir a la gravedad y se deslizaba colina abajo. Aunque la construcción resulta épica en su austeridad, presenta asimismo elementos cálidos: el jardín italianizante en el exterior y, en el interior, las inmensas chimeneas y las habitaciones con abundantes recuerdos y mobiliario testimonio de los siglos de tradición de la familia Cervini.

Scenes from garden and vineyard: spring buds; Livia and Anna, the two daughters of Leopoldo and Carolina Cervini; chestnuts in fall.

Immagini del giardino e della vigna: boccioli primaverili, Livia e Anna, le due figlie di Leopoldo e Carolina Cervini, e noccioli in autunno.

Szenen aus dem Garten und den Weinbergen: Frühlingsknospen; Livia und Anna, die beiden Töchter von Leopoldo und Carolina Cervini, sowie Kastanien im Herbst.

Quelques scènes du parc et du vignoble ; des bourgeons printaniers ; les deux filles de Leopoldo et Carolina Cervini, Livia et Anna, et des marrons à l'automne.

Escenas del jardín y los viñedos: retoños en primavera; las dos hijas de Leopoldo y Carolina Cervini, Livia y Anna; y castañas que caen al suelo.

Pucci

Palazzo Pucci, Firenze

The venerable Pucci name is woven into the history and culture of Tuscany, as well as the fashions of the world. Art works and artists are particularly linked with Pucci patronage, and works have been commissioned to commemorate their lives throughout history. Notably, the set of *spalliere* (painted wood) panels by Sandro Botticelli in 1483, based on Boccaccio's story of *Nastagio degli Onesti*, was created to honor the marriage of Giannozzo Pucci to Lucrezia Bini. Coats of arms of both families are visible in the panels, along with the coat of arms of the Medici family who is believed to have arranged the marriage. Being tied so closely to the life and history of Florence has some drawbacks as well. The family's painting of the *Martyrdom of Saint Sebastian* was created by the Pollaiolo brothers for the Pucci Chapel of the Church of the *Santissima Annunziata*. When the family decided to sell the painting (now in the National Gallery, London), citizen outrage resulted in a tribunal.

Il nobile nome dei Pucci è profondamente legato alla storia e alla cultura della Toscana, ma anche al mondo della moda. I Pucci sono particolarmente noti per essere stati grandi mecenati, e nel corso dei secoli sono state molte le opere commissionate per celebrarne le imprese. Le più straordinaria è rappresentata dalla serie di spalliere per letto di Sandro Botticelli, ispirate al *Nastagio degli Onesti* di Boccaccio e realizzate nel 1483 in occasione del matrimonio tra Giannozzo Pucci e Lucrezia Bini. I blasoni di entrambe le famiglie sono ben visibili sui pannelli, insieme allo stemma dei Medici (che si dice avessero organizzato le nozze). Un legame così stretto con la storia e la vita di Firenze ebbe però talvolta anche i suoi inconvenienti. Quando i Pucci decisero di vendere il *Martirio di San Sebastiano* (attualmente conservato alla *National Gallery* di Londra), realizzato dai fratelli Pollaiolo per la cappella di famiglia nella Chiesa della Santissima Annunziata, la cittadinanza indignata li trascinò in tribunale.

Der altehrwürdige Name Pucci ist nicht nur mit der Geschichte und Kultur der Toskana verwoben, sondern auch mit der Welt der Mode. Über die Jahrhunderte hinweg förderten die Puccis als Mäzene viele Kunstwerke und Künstler und erteilten zahlreiche Auftragsarbeiten, um ihrem Leben und Wirken ein Denkmal zu setzen. So malte zum Beispiel Sandro Botticelli im Jahr 1483 zu Ehren der Hochzeit von Giannozzo Pucci und Lucrezia Bini eine Gruppe von *Spalliere*-Tafelbildern mit Motiven aus Boccaccios Geschichte *Nastagio degli Onesti*. Die Familienwappen der beiden Linien sind auf den Gemälden zu erkennen, ebenso das Wappen der Medici, die vermutlich dieses Ehebündnis eingefädelt hatten. Die enge Verknüpfung des Familienlebens mit der Geschichte von Florenz hat allerdings auch seine Schattenseiten. Das berühmte Gemälde *Das Martyrium des Heiligen Sebastian* der Brüder Pollaiolo wurde für die Pucci-Kapelle in der Kirche *Santissima Annunziata* angefertigt. Als die Familie beschloss, dieses Kunstwerk zu veräußern (es hängt heute in der *National Gallery* in London), war die Empörung der Florentiner derart groß, dass es zu einem Prozess kam.

Le vénérable nom de Pucci est indissociable de l'histoire et de la culture de la Toscane et de la mode internationale. Les Pucci, en grands mécènes, n'ont cessé de soutenir des artistes et de commanditer des œuvres d'art pour rappeler leur vie tout au long de leur histoire. L'ensemble de *spalliere* (panneaux peints) réalisés par Sandro Botticelli en 1483, notamment, qui s'inspirent du *Nastagio degli Onesti*, histoire racontée par Boccace, commémore le mariage de Giannozzo Pucci et de Lucrezia Bini. Les blasons des deux familles sont visibles sur les panneaux, en compagnie des armes des Médicis qui – croit-on – arrangèrent le mariage. Ces liens si étroits avec la vie et l'histoire de Florence ont parfois présenté des inconvénients. La famille possédait un *Martyre de Saint Sébastien*, œuvre des frères Pollaiolo, qui ornait la chapelle de l'église de la *Santissima Annunziata*. Lorsqu'elle décida de le vendre (il est aujourd'hui conservé à la *National Gallery* à Londres), l'indignation des Florentins fut telle que l'affaire fut portée devant les tribunaux.

El venerable nombre de Pucci está tan entrelazado con la historia y la cultura de la Toscana, como al mundo de la moda. Numerosos artistas y sus trabajos están vinculados al patrocinio del clan Pucci, que ha encargado muchas obras en su historia para conmemorar celebraciones familiares. Entre ellas destacan los *spalliere* o casetones de madera pintados por Sandro Botticelli en 1483 con el título de *Nastagio degli Onesti*. El artista los creó con motivo del enlace matrimonial entre Giannozzo Pucci y Lucrezia Bini, inspirándose en un relato de Boccaccio. En dichos paneles aparecen también los escudos de armas de ambas familias, junto con el blasón heráldico de los Médicis quienes, al parecer, habían arreglado el compromiso. Pero tan estrechos vínculos con la vida y la historia de la ciudad de Florencia tienen también sus desventajas. La pintura propiedad de la familia *El martirio de san Sebastián* fue creada por los hermanos Pollaiolo para la capilla Pucci de la basílica de la *Santissima Annunziata*. Cuando los Pucci decidieron venderla (actualmente se encuentra en la *National Gallery* de Londres), la indignación ciudadana llegó a los tribunales.

Guarding the music room are two 17th century wooden Moors, a family motif. The Moors' bandanas display three symbols, originally hammers (the symbol of carpentry), that have evolved into the letter "T" to reflect the family motto: "Tempora, Tempera, Temporis" (Time reveals what is important).

Due mori in legno del XVII secolo, un motivo dello stemma del casato, sorvegliano la stanza della musica. La fascia dei mori reca tre simboli, in origine martelli, distintivo della carpenteria, poi evolutisi nella lettera "T", che rievoca il motto della famiglia: "Tempora, Tempera, Temporis" (Il tempo rivela ciò che è importante).

Das Musikzimmer wird von zwei hölzernen Mohren aus dem 17. Jahrhundert bewacht, dem Familiensymbol der Puccis. Auf den Stirnbändern der Mohren sieht man drei „T", die ursprünglich Hämmer waren (das Zeichen des Zimmermanns). Sie stehen für den Wahlspruch der Familie: „Tempora, Tempera, Temporis" (Die Zeit wird zeigen, was wichtig ist).

Deux Maures en bois datant du XVIIe siècle, un motif familial, montent la garde devant le salon de musique. Leurs bandeaux sont ornés de trois symboles, des marteaux à l'origine (symbole de la menuiserie), qui se sont mués en « T » pour se conformer à la devise familiale : « Tempora, Tempera, Temporis » (le temps révèle ce qui est important).

Dos moros (un motivo familiar) de madera del siglo XVII custodian la sala de música. En su bandana se aprecian tres simbólicos martillos (emblema de los carpinteros), que forman la letra "T" como alusión al lema de la familia: „Tempora, Tempera, Temporis" (El tiempo revela lo que es importante).

The family has taken refuge in Palazzo Pucci for centuries. Its rooftop and balcony boast one of the most intimate views of the *Duomo*. Within its walls is housed the Pucci archive, which not only documents the family's storied past, but has inspired contemporary design; in recent years, Emilio Pucci, the "Prince of Prints" design prints have come from designs in the archive. Giannozzo Pucci, whose editorial and publishing business is housed in the palace, has been active in bringing new life to the "natural" Florence, both by helping reinvigorate the Farmers' Market and helping connect Florence to its ecological traditions and the beautiful countryside that surrounds it.

La famiglia abita a Palazzo Pucci ormai da secoli. Dai suoi tetti e dalla balconata si gode di una delle viste più spettacolari del Duomo della città. Al suo interno si trova l'archivio Pucci, nel quale sono conservati i documenti riguardanti il passato ricco di storia del casato; esso rappresenta anche una fonte di ispirazione per la moda attuale; negli ultimi anni lo stilista Emilio Pucci, il cosiddetto "Prince of prints" per le sue collezioni si è ispirato proprio ai materiali contenuti nell'archivio. Il palazzo ospita anche la casa editrice di Giannozzo Pucci, impegnata nella valorizzazione di una Firenze in armonia con la natura, attraverso il sostegno ai mercati di prodotti locali e la riscoperta delle tradizioni ecologiche e della splendida campagna che circonda la città.

Die Familie hatte sich über die Jahrhunderte im Palazzo Pucci eingerichtet. Vom Dach und dem Balkon des Palastes hat man einen der schönsten Ausblicke auf den Florentiner Dom. Im Inneren des Palazzo findet man das Archiv der Pucci. Hier ist nicht nur die sagenumwobene Geschichte der Familie dokumentiert, sondern es inspirierte auch modernes Design. Emilio Pucci, der „Prince of Prints", hat sich immer wieder von den Entwürfen und Mustern im Archiv anregen lassen. Giannozzo Pucci, dessen Verlag heute im Palazzo untergebracht ist, setzt sich für ein „natürliches" Florenz ein. Er verhalf dem Bauernmarkt zu neuem Leben und ist darum bemüht, die Stadt wieder ihrer ökologischen Tradition und wunderschönen ländlichen Umgebung näher zu bringen.

La famille a trouvé un refuge dans le palais Pucci depuis des siècles. Son toit et son balcon offrent une vue tout à fait incomparable sur la cathédrale. Il abrite les archives Pucci, qui non seulement documentent le riche passé de la famille, mais ont marqué le design contemporain; Emilio Pucci, le « Prince de l'imprimé » y a en effet puisé son inspiration pour ses célèbres imprimés. Giannozzo Pucci, dont la maison d'édition a choisi le palais pour siège, a contribué à redonner vie à la Florence « naturelle », en aidant d'une part à imposer le marché des producteurs locaux et d'autre part, en faisant renaître les traditions écologiques de la ville, afin de la replacer dans le splendide cadre naturel qui est le sien.

El palacio Pucci ha sido el refugio de la familia durante siglos. La azotea y los balcones ofrecen una de las vistas más espectaculares del *Duomo*. Estas paredes dan cobijo al archivo de los Pucci, que no sólo custodia documentos del histórico pasado de la familia, sino que también ha servido de inspiración para el diseño contemporáneo. En los últimos años, Emilio Pucci, llamado el "príncipe del estampado", creó varios diseños inspirados en muestras de este archivo. Por su parte, Giannozzo Pucci, cuyo negocio editorial tiene su sede en el palacio, se ha comprometido con la labor de revivir la Florencia "natural", intentando recuperar los mercados de productos agrícolas de la zona y ayudando a que la ciudad se reencuentre con sus tradiciones ecológicas y la belleza del campo que la rodea.

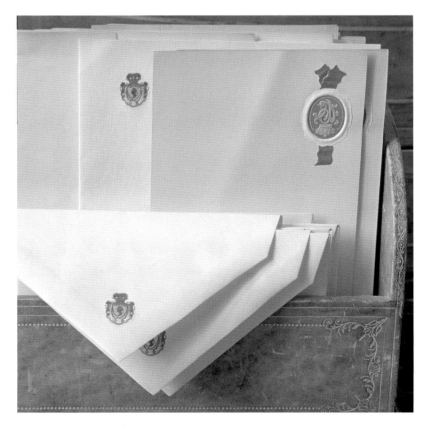

The palace's dining room, laid for tea, and a small sitting room in Empire style.

La sala da pranzo del palazzo, apparecchiata per il tè, e un piccolo salotto in stile Impero.

Das Esszimmer im Palast, für den Tee eingedeckt, und ein kleiner Salon im Empire-Stil.

La salle à manger du palais, où le couvert a été mis pour le thé, et un petit salon de style Empire.

El comedor de palacio, con servicio de té y una pequeña salita en estilo Imperio.

Antique spice jars line the shelves of an ornate cabinet. The two doorways lead into a gallery of paintings.

Antichi vasi per le spezie sugli scaffali di una credenza dai preziosi ornamenti. Dalle porte si accede a una galleria di dipinti.

Alte Gewürzgefäße schmücken die Regale eines kunstvoll gearbeiteten Kabinettschränkchens. Die zwei Durchgänge führen zu einer Gemäldegalerie.

Des pots à épices anciens bordent les étagères de cette vitrine somptueuse. Les deux portes ouvrent sur une galerie de peintures.

Antiguas jarras de especias alienadas en las estanterías de una recargada alacena. Las dos puertas conducen a la galería de las pinturas.

de Renzis Sonnino

Castello Sonnino, Montespertoli

Castello Sonnino, also widely known as Montespertoli Castle, has long been an intrinsic part of the outline and character of its namesake town. Originally the castle housed a church and cemetery; throughout the centuries, its artistic wealth bestowed many treasures on Montespertoli's surrounding churches and museums. Just outside of Florence, on the road of trade between Florence, Siena and Volterra, Castello Sonnino has been home to noble families for centuries. In 1393 the castle passed from the Lords of Montespertoli to the Machiavelli family. The Sonnino family took ownership in the early 19th century—Castello Sonnino was the longtime home to Prime Minister Baron Giorgio Sidney Sonnino (who also served intermittently from 1906 to 1919 as Foreign Minister and Minister of the Interior). Part of his archive is still housed in the castle.

Castello Sonnino, conosciuto anche come Castello di Montespertoli, è ormai considerato parte integrante del paesaggio e dello spirito del paese da cui prende il nome. Originariamente il complesso ospitava una chiesa con cimitero. Il suo patrimonio di opere d'arte, vecchio di secoli, è in gran parte rintracciabile oggi nei musei e nelle chiese dei dintorni di Montespertoli. Castello Sonnino, situato appena fuori Firenze sullo snodo commerciale tra il capoluogo toscano, Siena e Volterra, è stato per tempo immemorabile la dimora di molte famiglie nobili. Nel 1393 la proprietà del castello passò dai signori di Montespertoli ai Machiavelli. La famiglia Sonnino lo acquistò all'inizio del XIX secolo. Il castello fu per molti anni la residenza del primo ministro e barone Giorgio Sidney Sonnino (che dal 1906 al 1919 ricoprì in momenti successivi anche la carica di ministro degli Esteri e degli Interni). Parte del suo archivio personale è ancor oggi conservato all'interno dell'edificio.

Castello Sonnino, auch bekannt als Castello di Montespertoli, prägt Gesicht und Charakter des Städtchens, das ebenfalls den Namen Montespertoli trägt. Ursprünglich befanden sich im Schloss eine Kirche und ein Friedhof; über die Jahrhunderte bescherte der künstlerische Reichtum des Schlosses den anliegenden Kirchen und Museen in Montespertoli immer wieder zahlreiche Schätze. Gelegen ist es kurz vor Florenz auf der Handelsstraße zwischen Florenz, Siena und Volterra und beherbergte seit seiner Gründung viele verschiedene Adelsfamilien. 1393 ging es beispielsweise von den Herren von Montespertoli in den Besitz der Machiavellis über. Die Familie Sonnino übernahm es im frühen 19. Jahrhundert. So wurde das Schloss zum Heim des Ministerpräsidenten Baron Giorgio Sidney Sonnino (der zwischen 1906 bis 1919 auch zeitweise als Außen- und Innenminister fungierte). Teile seines Archivs befinden sich heute noch im Schloss.

Castello Sonnino, bien connu aussi sous le nom de château de Montespertoli, est depuis longtemps un élément intrinsèque de la silhouette et du caractère de la ville éponyme. À l'origine, il abritait une église et un cimetière ; au fil des siècles, il a fait profiter de ses richesses artistiques les églises et les musées des environs de Montespertoli. Situé juste aux abords de Florence, sur la route commerciale reliant Florence, Sienne et Volterra, Castello Sonnino est une demeure noble depuis des siècles. En 1393, il passa des seigneurs de Montespertoli aux Machiavelli. Les Sonnino s'y installèrent au début du XIXe siècle – le baron Giorgio Sidney Sonnino, qui fut premier ministre, y résida longuement (il fut en outre ministre des Affaires étrangères et ministre de l'Intérieur à plusieurs reprises, entre 1906 et 1919). Une partie de ses archives est conservée ici.

Castello Sonnino, más conocido como castillo Montespertoli, ha sido parte intrínseca de la línea del horizonte y el carácter de la ciudad del mismo nombre. Originalmente, el complejo tenía una iglesia con cementerio. A través de los siglos, su riqueza artística ofreció muchos tesoros a las iglesias y museos de los alrededores. Situado en las afueras de Florencia, en la ruta comercial entre Florencia, Siena y Volterra, el castillo Sonnino ha sido la residencia de familias nobles durante siglos. En 1393, la construcción pasó de los señores de Montespertoli a la familia Maquiavelo. El linaje Sonnino se hizo con su propiedad a principios del siglo XIX. El castillo fue durante largo tiempo el hogar del primer ministro, el barón Giorgio Sidney Sonnino, quien también alternó los cargos de ministro de asuntos exteriores y ministro de interior de 1906 a 1919. Parte de su archivo personal se conserva aún en el castillo.

Bust and sketches from the collection of Giorgio Sidney Sonnino. Castello Sonnino houses important documents relating to Italy's involvement in World War I, as well as to the Paris and Versailles Conferences.

Busto e schizzi dalla collezione di Giorgio Sidney Sonnino. Il castello Sonnino conserva importanti documenti relativi alla partecipazione italiana alla prima guerra mondiale e alle conferenze di Parigi e di Versailles.

Büste und Skizzen aus der Sammlung von Giorgio Sidney Sonnino. Das Castello Sonnino beherbergt wichtige Dokumente zur Rolle Italiens während des Ersten Weltkriegs und der Pariser und Versailler Konferenz.

Bustes et dessins de la collection de Giorgio Sidney Sonnino. Le Castello Sonnino abrite d'importants documents concernant le rôle de l'Italie dans la Première Guerre mondiale et les Conférences de Paris et de Versailles.

Busto y bocetos de la colección de Giorgio Sidney Sonnino. El castillo Sonnino acoge importantes documentos referentes a la participación de Italia en la Primera Guerra Mundial, así como en las conferencias de París y Versalles.

While the castle is historically of interest and serves as a community landmark, it also has a more private dimension—that of family home and business center for the de Renzis Sonnino family. The house, with its proportions and balanced exterior and interior space, creates a comfortable home. Though the tower has been rebuilt, the house is in its original condition and has revealed passages and hidden tunnels to the family; for example, the exit from the church was discovered and subsequently converted. The castle also houses the Baron Alessandro's shop and tasting room for the wine and olive oil business. The Baroness Caterina studied at New York's Pratt Institute and enjoys a successful career as a wine label designer.

Il castello rappresenta un luogo di grande interesse storico e viene considerato il simbolo della comunità, ma possiede anche una dimensione più privata: è infatti l'abitazione e la sede dell'azienda della famiglia de Renzis Sonnino. L'edificio, grazie all'armonia delle proporzioni e di tutti i suoi spazi, sia interni che esterni, trasmette un piacevole senso d'accoglienza. La torre fortificata è stata ricostruita, ma il palazzo del castello ha mantenuto la conformazione originale, rivelando ai suoi abitanti numerosi passaggi e gallerie segrete; tra questi è riaffiorata quella che era l'uscita dalla chiesa, poi adibita ad altro uso. Il castello ospita anche il locale del barone Alessandro per la vendita diretta e la degustazione dei vini e degli oli dell'azienda. La baronessa Caterina ha studiato alla *Pratt Institute* di New York, svolge con successo la professione di fotografa e designer di etichette e loghi di case vinicole.

Das Castello ist nicht nur historisch interessant und gilt als Wahrzeichen des Ortes, sondern besitzt auch privatere Aspekte – es dient als Familien- und Geschäftssitz der de Renzis Sonninos. Das Gebäude, mit seinen klaren Linien im inneren und äußeren Erscheinungsbild, weist behagliche Dimensionen auf. Außer dem Turm, der neu errichtet werden musste, befindet es sich in seinem ursprünglichen Bauzustand und enthüllt der Familie immer wieder verborgene Zugänge und Tunnel; so wurde zum Beispiel der Kirchenausgang eines Tages wiederentdeckt und umgebaut. Im Schloss befinden sich auch die Probierstube und der Verkaufsraum des Baron Alessandro de Renzis Sonnino, wo man Weine und Olivenöl erwerben kann. Die Baronin Caterina studierte am New Yorker *Pratt Institute* und entwirft mit Erfolg Weinetiketten.

Si le château présente un intérêt historique et sert de phare à la communauté, il possède par ailleurs une dimension plus intime – celle de demeure familiale et de siège des activités économiques des de Renzis Sonnino. L'équilibre de ses proportions, l'harmonie entre extérieurs et intérieurs, en font une habitation confortable. Bien que la tour ait été reconstruite, la demeure se trouve dans son état d'origine. La famille y a découvert des passages secrets et des tunnels cachés, ainsi un souterrain partant de l'église, qui a été converti ensuite. En outre, le château accueille la boutique et la salle de dégustation des vins et des huiles d'olives fabriqués par l'entreprise du baron Alessandro. La barone Caterina, qui a étudié au *Pratt Institute* de New York, conçoit des étiquettes de vin qui remportent le plus grand succès.

Aunque el edificio tiene interés histórico y es un emblema de la comunidad, también está dotado de una dimensión privada, ya que constituye la residencia familiar y sede de los negocios del clan de Renzis Sonnino. La casa, con sus proporcionados y equilibrados espacios exteriores e interiores desprende un ambiente hogareño muy acogedor. Aunque la torre ha sido reconstruida, el edificio se conserva en su estado original y ha revelado pasajes y túneles ocultos a la familia; así por ejemplo, se descubrió una salida desde la iglesia que fue convenientemente restaurada. El castillo acoge asimismo la tienda y la sala de degustación del negocio de vinos y aceite de oliva que regenta el barón Alessandro. Por su parte, la baronesa Caterina estudió en el *Pratt Institute* de Nueva York y disfruta de una exitosa carrera como diseñadora de etiquetas de vinos.

Baron Alessandro de Renzis Sonnino, the Baroness Caterina, and their two children, Virginia and Leone.

Il barone Alessandro de Renzis Sonnino con la baronessa Caterina e i due figli, Virginia e Leone.

Baron Alessandro de Renzis Sonnino, Baroness Caterina und ihre beiden Kinder Virginia und Leone.

Le baron Alessandro de Renzis Sonnino, la baronne Caterina et leurs deux enfants, Virginia et Leone.

El barón Alessandro de Renzis Sonnino, la baronesa Caterina y sus dos hijos, Virginia y Leone.

Two salons: trompe l'œil creates formal architectural details in one salon and transports the Yellow Salon to somewhere north of Tuscany with its encompassing, early 1800s design.

Due saloni: la decorazione trompe l'œil crea elementi architettonici formali in un ambiente e con il suo stile primo Ottocento pare trasportare altrove il salotto giallo, in un luogo imprecisato a nord della Toscana.

Zwei Salons: in einem Salon spiegelt ein Trompe-l'Œil architektonische Details vor, und im Gelben Salon vermittelt die Gestaltung aus dem frühen 19. Jahrhundert den Eindruck, man befände sich nördlich der Toskana.

Deux salons : dans l'un, un trompe-l'œil crée des détails architecturaux formels et, avec sa décoration début XIXe, transporte le salon jaune quelque part au nord de la Toscane.

Dos salones: los frescos trompe l'œil crean detalles arquitectónicos formales en una de las salas y transportan el Salón amarillo a algún lugar del norte de la Toscana con su diseño de principios del siglo XIX.

The view from the tower into the courtyard and beyond to the town of Montespertoli with its renowned countryside. The farm currently consisting of 500 acre, produces wines including Chianti Montespertoli DOCG, Sangiovese, and Vin Santo, as well as Grappa and extra virgin olive oil.

Vista dalla torre sul cortile, il paese di Montespertoli e il suo celebre paesaggio. La tenuta si estende su 200 ettari e produce vini, fra cui il Chianti Montespertoli DOCG, Sangiovese e Vin Santo, oltre a grappa e olio extra vergine di oliva.

Der Blick vom Turm aus in den Innenhof und zum Städtchen Montespertoli mit seiner berühmten Landschaft. Das Gut umfasst zur Zeit 200 Hektar Boden, auf dem Weine wie der Chianti Montespertoli DOCG, Sangiovese und Vin Santo sowie Grappa und kaltgepresstes Olivenöl produziert werden.

Vue de la tour sur la cour et au-delà, sur la ville de Montespertoli et sa campagne renommée. L'exploitation agricole, qui couvre actuellement 200 hectares, produit des vins, dont du chianti montespertoli DOCG, du sangiovese et du vin santo, de même que de la grappa et de l'huile d'olive vierge extra.

Vista desde la torre sobre el patio con la ciudad de Montespertoli y su renombrado paisaje al fondo. La granja tiene actualmente 200 hectáreas y produce vino, entre otros, Chianti Montespertoli DOCG, Sangiovese y Vin Santo, así como grappa y aceite de oliva virgen extra.

della Gherardesca

Castello della Gherardesca, Castagneto Carducci

The della Gherardesca castle, which dates back to the year one thousand, is still inhabited by the della Gherardesca family. This ancient family exemplifies the strife that engulfed Tuscany in Medieval and Renaissance times. Count Ugolino della Gherardesca, a Guelf (pro-papal) leader in predominantly Ghibelline (pro-imperial) Pisa, in 1284 attempted to strike an accord between the two factions. He failed, and his enemies conspired against him. As related in Dante's *Inferno*, he was shut in a tower with his sons to starve to death. This castle, situated on Tuscany's coast south of Pisa, had been within Pisa's territory from the 1100s, but in 1406, the Counts of della Gherardesca switched allegiances, turning to the protection of Florence. In turn, they were put in charge of many area hamlets of the area, which continued until 1749.

Il Castello della Gherardesca, che risale all'anno mille, è ancor oggi abitato dalla famiglia da cui prende il nome. Questo antico casato può essere considerato un simbolo delle lotte che dilaniarono la Toscana in epoca medievale e rinascimentale. Il conte Ugolino della Gherardesca, signore guelfo in una Pisa a maggioranza ghibellina, nel 1284 cercò un'alleanza con la fazione avversa, ma finì per cadere in una congiura dei suoi nemici. Come Dante ci descrive nel suo *Inferno*, il conte verrà rinchiuso in una torre insieme ai figli e condannato alla morte per inedia. Il castello, situato sulla costa toscana a sud di Pisa, faceva parte del territorio della città sin dal XII secolo. Nel 1406, i conti della Gherardesca sciolsero la vecchia alleanza con la città e passarono dalla parte di Firenze. In cambio ottennero un dominio che si estendeva su diversi villaggi della zona e che durò fino al 1749.

Das Schloss della Gherardesca, dessen Wurzeln ins Jahr 1000 zurückreichen, wird auch heute noch von der Familie della Gherardesca bewohnt. In der Geschichte dieser alten Familie spiegelt sich deutlich der Kampf wider, der im Mittelalter und der Renaissance um die Toskana ausgetragen wurde. Graf Ugolino della Gherardesca, der Anführer der Guelfen (Unterstützer des Papstes) im von den Ghibellinen (Unterstützer des Kaisers) beherrschten Pisa war, versuchte 1284 einen Kompromiss zwischen den beiden Fraktionen auszuhandeln. Es misslang ihm jedoch und seine Feinde verschworen sich daraufhin gegen ihn. Dante griff dessen Schicksal später in seinem *Inferno* auf, in dem er schildert, wie der Graf gemeinsam mit seinen Söhnen in einen Turm eingekerkert wurde und elendig sterben musste. Das Schloss, das an der toskanischen Küste südlich von Pisa liegt, befand sich seit dem 12. Jahrhundert auf dem Territorium der Stadt Pisa. 1406 brachen die Grafen della Gherardesca die Allianz und wandten sich Florenz zu. Als Dank erhielten sie zahlreiche Ortschaften in der Gegend als Lehen, die sie bis 1749 hielten.

Les della Gherardesca continuent à vivre dans le château éponyme, qui remonte à l'an mil. Cette famille très ancienne incarne les luttes qui ensanglantèrent la Toscane au Moyen Âge et à la Renaissance. Le comte Ugolino della Gherardesca, chef de file des Guelfes (partisans du pape) dans une Pise surtout gibeline (pour l'empereur), tenta en 1284 de trouver un accord entre les deux factions. Il échoua et ses ennemis conspirèrent contre lui. Dante raconte dans son *Enfer* qu'il fut condamné à être enfermé dans une tour avec ses fils et à y mourir de faim. Ce château, situé sur la côte toscane au sud de Pise, se trouvait sur le territoire pisan depuis le XIIᵉ siècle, mais, en 1406, les comtes della Gherardesca changèrent d'alliances et se placèrent sous la protection de Florence. En échange, ils devinrent seigneurs de nombreux villages de la région, jusqu'en 1749.

El castillo della Gherardesca, en pie desde el año 1000, está aún habitado por la familia del mismo apellido. Este linaje de rancio abolengo ejemplifica perfectamente los conflictos que marcaron la Toscana durante la Edad Media y el Renacimiento. El conde Ugolino della Gherardesca, un líder güelfo (fiel al Papa), que residía en Pisa, (ciudad predominantemente gibelina o pro-imperial), intentó en 1284 que ambas partes llegaran a un acuerdo. Pero falló en el intento y sus enemigos conspiraron contra él. Tal y como Dante relata en su *Infierno*, lo encerraron bajo llave en una torre junto con sus hijos hasta que murieron de hambre. Ese castillo, situado en las tierras litorales del sur de Pisa, pasó a formar parte de la demarcación de la ciudad del siglo XII, pero en el año 1406, los condes de della Gherardesca cambiaron de aliados y volvieron a acogerse a la protección de Florencia. A cambio, se les otorgó de varios caseríos de la zona, situación que continuó hasta 1749.

An ornate nativity scene is displayed in preparation for Christmas. Two busts of various counts of Donoratico flank a salon. A cast model of Carpeaux's "Ugolino and his Sons" depicts one of this family's most tragic stories.

Un ricco presepio per celebrare il Natale. Due busti dei conti di Donoratico ai lati del salone. Copia dell'opera di Carpeaux "Ugolino e i suoi figli", che illustra una delle storie più tragiche della famiglia.

Zu Weihnachten wird eine große Krippe aufgestellt. Zwei Büsten der Grafen von Donoratico schmücken einen Salon. Ein Abguss von Carpeaux' „Ugolino und seine Söhne" erinnert an eine der großen Familientragödien.

Une magnifique crèche a été installée pour Noël. De chaque côté du salon, un buste des comtes de Donoratico. Un moulage de « l'Ugolin et ses fils » de Carpeaux illustre l'un des épisodes les plus tragiques de l'histoire familiale.

Un recargado nacimiento se expone como preparación para la Navidad. Dos bustos de los condes de Donoratico flanquean el salón. La réplica en escayola de la escultura "Ugolino y sus hijos" de Carpeaux representa una de las historias más trágicas de esta familia.

The three children of Guelfo della Gherardesca: Gaddo, Manfredi and Sibilla, have harmoniously blended a thousand years of history, Tuscan relics and modern art into a comfortable home.

Gaddo, Manfredi e Sibilla, i tre figli di Guelfo della Gherardesca, hanno saputo unire armoniosamente una storia millenaria, antichità toscane e arte moderna in un casa ospitale e confortevole.

Die drei Kinder von Guelfo della Gherardesca: Gaddo, Manfredi und Sibilla verbinden souverän eine tausendjährige Geschichte, toskanische Antiquitäten und moderne Kunst zu einem behaglichen Zuhause.

Gaddo, Manfredi et Sibilla, les trois enfants de Guelfo della Gherardesca, ont su allier avec harmonie, dans une demeure confortable, une histoire millénaire, des reliques toscanes et des œuvres d'art moderne.

Los tres hijos de Guelfo della Gherardesca: Gaddo, Manfredi y Sibilla han sabido mezclar armoniosamente mil años de historia, reliquias toscanas y arte moderno en un confortable hogar.

The della Gherardesca castle is situated at the end of a road that winds its way through and encompasses Castagneto Carducci. A medieval town, Castagneto replaced its former "surname" of Marittimo with the name of Carducci in 1907 to honor the poet Giosuè Carducci, who had been awarded the Nobel Prize for Literature in 1906. Carducci had visited and been inspired by Castagneto Marittimo as a young man, and his poem *Before San Guido* immortalized neighboring hamlet Bolgheri's cypress alley. Today, Guelfo della Gherardesca and his children have been inspired to diligently restore Castagneto's castle, the hub of this busy family. Careful updates are visible in every room, and the family has invigorated the design with special touches, such as an occasional piece of modern art among the period furniture. The peaceful courtyard and crenellated walls look over the town to the Maremma countryside and the Mediterranean Sea beyond.

Il Castello della Gherardesca sorge in fondo a una strada che attraversa e circonda Castagneto Carducci. La cittadina di epoca medievale ha cambiato il suo "cognome" originale da Marittimo a Carducci nel 1907, in onore del poeta Giosuè, insignito del premio Nobel per la letteratura nel 1906. Carducci aveva visitato Castagneto Marittimo in gioventù, traendone ispirazione, e nella composizione *Davanti San Guido* aveva immortalato il viale di cipressi del vicino borgo di Bolgheri. Gli attuali padroni, Guelfo della Gherardesca e i suoi figli, sono stati artefici di una sapiente opera di restauro del castello di Castagneto, centro nevralgico dell'attività di famiglia. Ogni sala presenta ben visibili i segni di questa ristrutturazione, e la famiglia ha aggiunto qua e là alcuni tocchi personali, come inattese opere d'arte moderna che fanno capolino tra i mobili d'epoca. Dal suo placido cortile e dalle mura merlate si possono dominare la città e la campagna maremmana, fino al Mar Mediterraneo.

Das Schloss della Gherardesca liegt am Ende einer Straße, die sich um und durch Castagneto Carducci schlängelt. Castagneto ist eine mittelalterliche Stadt, die 1907 ihren ursprünglich zweiten Namensteil Marittimo durch Carducci ersetzte, um damit den Dichter Giosuè Carducci zu ehren, der 1906 den Nobelpreis für Literatur erhielt. Carducci hatte als junger Mann Castagneto Marittimo besucht und sich von diesem Ort inspirieren lassen. So verewigte er zum Beispiel in seinem Gedicht *Vor San Guido* die Zypressenallee des benachbarten Örtchen Bolgheri. Guelfo della Gherardesca und seine Kinder haben sich in heutiger Zeit die Aufgabe gesetzt, das Schloss in Castagneto sorgfältig zu restaurieren. Schließlich bildet es den Lebensmittelpunkt der geschäftigen Familie. So lassen sich in jedem Raum gewissenhaft ausgeführte Veränderungen erkennen, und die Familie ist darum bemüht, die alten Gemäuer auch mit modernen Kunstgegenständen zu beleben, die zwischen den antiken Möbeln arrangiert sind. Das Schloss, mit dem stillen Innenhof und den mit Zinnen versehenen Mauern, erhebt sich über der Stadt und bietet einen Ausblick auf die Maremma und das dahinterliegende Mittelmeer.

Le château della Gherardesca est situé à la fin d'une route tortueuse qui passe par Castagneto Carducci. Le village médiéval de Castagneto remplaça son ancien « surnom » de Marittimo par le nom de Carducci en 1907, en hommage au poète Giosuè Carducci qui reçut le prix Nobel de littérature en 1906. Dans sa jeunesse, Carducci s'était rendu à Castagneto Marittimo qui lui avait inspiré un poème, *Devant San Guido*, où il immortalisa l'allée de cyprès du village voisin de Bolgheri. Aujourd'hui, Guelfo della Gherardesca et ses enfants ont été bien inspirés de restaurer avec soin le château de Castagneto, berceau de cette famille entreprenante. Chaque pièce a bénéficié de retouches judicieuses et de notes particulières qui en affinent le design, ainsi ces œuvres d'art moderne qui pimentent le mobilier ancien. La cour paisible et les murs à créneaux offrent une belle vue sur la Maremme et le paysage méditerranéen.

El castillo della Gherardesca se encuentra al final de la carretera serpenteante que rodea la localidad de Castagneto Carducci. Esta ciudad medieval, cambió su antiguo apelativo de Marittimo por el de Carducci en 1907 en honor al poeta Giosuè Carducci, galardonado con el premio Nobel de literatura en 1906. Carducci había visitado la ciudad de Castagneto Marittimo y se había dejado inspirar por ella en su juventud. En su poema *Delante de San Guido*, inmortalizó el paseo de cipreses de la vecina aldea de Bolgheri. Hoy en día, Guelfo della Gherardesca y sus hijos han llevado a cabo una diligente restauración del castillo, centro neurálgico de la actividad de la familia. Las cuidadosas remodelaciones se aprecian en cada habitación; la familia ha reforzado el diseño con toques especiales como una ocasional pieza de arte moderno en medio del mobiliario de época. El apacible patio y sus muros almenados miran sobre la ciudad hacia las tierras costeras de Maremma con el Mediterráneo de fondo.

The portrait of Giulia della Gherardesca hangs in the 19ᵗʰ century salon. A mirror reflects Manfredi della Gherardesca's canopied bed.

Il ritratto di Giulia della Gherardesca nella sala del XIX secolo. Uno specchio riflette il letto a baldacchino di Manfredi della Gherardesca.

Das Porträt von Giulia della Gherardesca im Salon aus dem 19. Jahrhundert. Im Spiegel kann man das Bett mit Baldachin von Manfredi della Gherardesca sehen.

Dans le salon XIXᵉ portrait de Giulia della Gherardesca. Un miroir reflète le lit à baldaquin de Manfredi della Gherardesca.

El retrato de Giulia della Gherardesca cuelga en el salón decimonónico. Un espejo refleja la cama con dosel de Manfredi della Gherardesca.

The salon's floor is cotto impruneta and marble; Salotto Affrescato is so named due to the extensive trompe l'œil covering the walls and ceiling.

Il pavimento della stanza è di marmo e cotto impruneta; le pareti e il soffitto sono decorati da un trompe l'œil, da cui la definizione "Salotto Affrescato".

Der Boden im Salon ist aus Cotto Impruneta und Marmor, das große Trompe-l'Œil, das Wände und die Decke schmückt, gab dem Salotto Affrescato den Namen.

Le sol du salon est en cotto impruneta et en marbre. Le Salotto Affrescato doit son nom au vaste trompe-l'œil qui couvre les murs et le plafond.

El suelo del salón es de cotto impruneta y mármol. El Salotto Affrescato es llamado así debido al magnífico trompe l'œil que cubre las paredes y el techo.

Mazzei

Castello di Fonterutoli, Castellina in Chianti

The wine-making Mazzei family dates back to the 11th century in Carmignano (a town well known for its wine prominence). The Fonterutoli property came into the Mazzei family through marriage in 1435, and became part of this family's visionary wine heritage. The family's history of deepening its wine knowledge and then sharing that accumulated expertise goes back centuries. Filippo Mazzei (1730–1816) went to America to consult with Thomas Jefferson on his vineyard in Virginia, and stayed to fight in the American Revolutionary War. Lapo Mazzei, the current owner of Fonterutoli, has promoted the wines of the region and led the effort to improve both their quality and reputation during his 20-year tenure as president of the Chianti Classico Consortium (having served since 1974 on the board and for ten years as vice president). Lapo's sons, Filippo and Francesco, continue to reach out beyond their own winery by working with other Chianti producers as well as modernizing their own production.

L'origine dei Mazzei, una famiglia di viticoltori, risale all'XI secolo a Carmignano, un paese con una grande tradizione di vini di qualità. Il casato acquisì il Castello di Fonterutoli nel 1435 grazie a un matrimonio e lo rese parte integrante del suo grande progetto di produzione vinicola. La storia di famiglia è caratterizzata dagli studi approfonditi sulle tecniche di lavorazione del vino e sulla condivisione con gli altri produttori di questa loro ormai centenaria esperienza. Filippo Mazzei (1730–1816) si recò addirittura in America per consigliare Thomas Jefferson riguardo ai suoi vigneti in Virginia, e rimase coinvolto nella Guerra d'indipendenza americana. Lapo Mazzei, l'attuale proprietario di Fonterutoli, nei suoi vent'anni di servizio per il Consorzio Chianti Classico in qualità di presidente (ne ha fatto parte fin dal 1974, prima come membro del consiglio e poi, per dieci anni, come vicepresidente), si è preoccupato di diffondere il buon nome dei vini della regione promuovendone il continuo miglioramento qualitativo. I figli di Lapo, Filippo e Francesco, continuano a espandere l'azienda, non solo collaborando con altri produttori del Chianti, ma anche applicando le tecnologie più moderne.

Die Wurzeln der Weinproduzenten Mazzei lassen sich in Carmignano (eine Stadt, die für ihre Weine berühmt ist) bis ins 11. Jahrhundert zurück-verfolgen. 1435 gelangte das Castello di Fonterutoli durch eine Heirat in den Besitz der Familie und wurde so zu einem wichtigen Teil ihres zukünf-tigen Weingutes. Die Familie hat seit Jahrhunderten ihr Wissen um den Weinbau vertieft und diese Kenntnisse mit anderen geteilt. Filippo Mazzei (1730–1816) reiste sogar bis nach Amerika, um Thomas Jefferson hinsichtlich seines Weinberges in Virginia zu beraten, und blieb dann gleich dort, um im amerikanischen Unabhängigkeitskrieg mitzukämpfen. Lapo Mazzei, der augenblickliche Besitzer von Fonterutoli, hat während seiner 20 Jahre langen Präsidentschaft des Chianti-Classico-Consortiums die Weine der Region gefördert und sowohl ihre Qualität als auch ihren Ruf enorm verbessert (seit 1974 sitzt er im Vorstand und war zehn Jahre lang Vizepräsident). Lapo Mazzeis Söhne Filippo und Francesco setzen die Tradition des Vaters fort. Sie arbeiten eng mit anderen Chianti-Produzenten zusammen und sind stets bemüht, die Produktion zu modernisieren.

Les Mazzei, une grande famille de viticulteurs, habitent depuis le XIe siècle à Carmignano, ville fort connue pour ses vins superbes. Par un mariage célébré en 1435, ils acquièrent le château de Fonterutoli qui devint une partie intégrante de l'héritage viticole visionnaire de la famille. Depuis des siècles, celle-ci cultive la tradition de la connaissance du vin et du partage de son expertise. Filippo Mazzei (1730–1816), qui partit en Amérique afin de consulter Thomas Jefferson sur ses vignes de Virginie, y resta pour participer à la guerre de l'Indépendance américaine. Lapo Mazzei, propriétaire actuel de Fonterutoli, a assuré la promotion des vins de la région et œuvré pour améliorer tant leur qualité que leur réputation au cours de ses 20 ans de présidence du Consortium Chianti Classico (il fait partie du conseil depuis 1974 et fut vice-président pendant dix ans). Les fils de Lapo, Filippo et Francesco, continuent à dépasser les limites de leur exploitation en collaborant avec d'autres producteurs du Chianti mais aussi en modernisant leur propre production.

Las primeras noticias del clan de vinateros Mazzei datan del siglo XI en la localidad de Carmignano, conocida por la excelencia de sus vinos. La propiedad Fonterutoli pasó a manos de los Mazzei por un matrimonio celebrado en el año 1435, con lo que se añadió al legado de estos visionarios productores de vinos. La historia de esta familia que siempre ha dependido de los conocimientos sobre el vino y ha compartido la experiencia acumulada se remonta a siglos atrás. Filippo Mazzei (1730–1816) viajó a Norteamérica con la intención de consultar a Thomas Jefferson sobre sus viñedos de Virginia y se quedó para combatir en la Guerra de Independencia de EE.UU. Lapo Mazzei, el actual propietario de Fonterutoli, ha promocionado los vinos de la región y ha dirigido sus esfuerzos a mejorar su reputación y calidad durante los veinte años en el cargo de presidente del Chianti Classico Consortium (habiendo siendo miembro de la junta desde 1974 y diez años vicepresidente). Los hijos de Lapo, Filippo y Francesco, siguen intentando llegar más allá de los límites del negocio familiar trabajando con otros productores de Chianti y modernizando su propia explotación.

The brothers Filippo and Francesco Mazzei, involved in the daily workings of the estate, pictured here on a terrace of the house.

I fratelli Filippo e Francesco Mazzei, che si occupano dei lavori quotidiani della tenuta, qui ritratti su una terrazza della casa.

Die Brüder Filippo und Francesco Mazzei, mit den täglichen Geschäften des Guts beschäftigt, hier auf der Terrasse ihres Anwesens.

Les frères Filippo et Francesco Mazzei, qui participent au travail quotidien de la propriété, représentés ici sur la terrasse de la demeure.

Los hermanos Filippo y Francesco Mazzei, involucrados en las tareas cotidianas de la hacienda, en una terraza de la casa.

Castello di Fonterutoli   *Castellina in Chianti*   213

The hamlet of Fonterutoli is situated along the historically contended Siena–Florence border, and served as the location for the signing of a 13th century peace treaty. This accord determined that the Chianti wine area should be part of the Republic of Florence and resulted in the black rooster becoming the symbol of Chianti wine. Castello di Fonterutoli was originally a place to change horses on the road from Siena to Florence. In the 16th century, Senator Giovanni Mazzei added a second floor to transform the building into a residence. The house epitomizes a working country home, devoid of excesses and focused on the land outside its windows, where the family's work is centered.

Il borgo di Fonterutoli è situato sul travagliato confine tra Siena e Firenze. Nel XIII secolo ha ospitato la firma di un trattato di pace tra le due città. Con quell'accordo la regione vinicola del Chianti divenne un possedimento della Repubblica di Firenze e, da allora, il gallo nero è diventato il simbolo dei suoi vini. Il Castello di Fonterutoli era in origine una stazione per il cambio dei cavalli sulla strada tra Siena e Firenze. Nel XVI secolo il senatore Giovanni Mazzei fece aggiungere un secondo piano per trasformare l'edificio in residenza. L'edificio è un perfetto esempio di casa-azienda rurale, priva di fronzoli e schietta come la terra che la circonda e che rappresenta il cuore dell'attività di famiglia.

Das Örtchen Fonterutoli liegt auf der historisch bedeutsamen Grenzlinie Siena–Florenz, weshalb dort auch ein Friedensvertrag im 13. Jahrhundert unterzeichnet wurde. Darin hieß es u. a., dass die Chianti-Region der Republik Florenz zugeteilt wird – eine politische Zugehörigkeit, die sich auch in dem schwarzen Hahn niederschlägt, dem Symbol des Chianti-Weines. Die Villa Fonterutoli diente ursprünglich zum Wechseln der Pferde auf dem Weg von Siena nach Florenz. Im 16. Jahrhundert ließ der Senator Giovanni Mazzei dann ein weiteres Stockwerk hinzufügen, um das Gebäude in ein Wohnhaus zu verwandeln. Das Haus stellt ein typisches, voll funktionstüchtiges Landhaus dar, in dem es keine überflüssigen Dekorationen gibt, sondern das ganz und gar auf das umliegende Land ausgerichtet scheint, wo die Familie tätig ist.

Le village de Fonterutoli, situé sur la frontière longtemps contestée entre Sienne et Florence, accueillit les signataires d'un traité de paix au XIIIe siècle. D'après cet accord, le vignoble du Chianti devait faire partie de la République de Florence et le coq noir devenir le symbole de ses vins. Le château Fonterutoli était à l'origine une poste où les voyageurs changeaient de chevaux sur la route de Sienne à Florence. Au XVIe siècle, le sénateur Giovanni Mazzei fit construire un deuxième étage pour transformer l'édifice en résidence. La demeure symbolise la propriété rurale industrieuse, refusant tout excès et se concentrant sur la campagne visible de ses fenêtres, là où travaille la famille.

La estancia de Fonterutoli está situada en los históricamente disputados límites entre Siena y Florencia, y sirvió de emplazamiento para la firma del tratado de paz del siglo XIII. Este acuerdo determinó que el área del vino de Chianti debía ser parte de la República de Florencia; como consecuencia, el gallo negro pasó a ser el símbolo del vino de Chianti. Villa Fonterutoli era originalmente un lugar en el que abrevar y refrescar los caballos junto a la senda que unía Siena y Florencia. En el siglo XVI el senador Giovanni Mazzei añadió un segundo piso para transformar el edificio en una residencia. La casa reúne todas las características de una hacienda rústica; evita cualquier exceso y se abre desde sus ventanales a los campos en los que se centra la labor de la familia.

In Lapo's study hangs the framed letter (1780) from Leopoldo, Grand Duke of Tuscany, honoring the family. Entrance with coat of arms inscribed with the phrase "Misericordia (mercy / compassion) from generation to generation to the one who fears Him."

Nello studio di Lapo è appesa, incorniciata, la lettera del 1780 del Granduca Leopoldo di Toscana, in cui si onora la famiglia. Entrata con stemma e motto: "Misericordia di generazione in generazione per chi ha timore di Lui".

In Lapo Mazzeis Arbeitszimmer hängt der Brief des toskanischen Großherzogs Leopold von 1780, mit dem dieser der Familie die Ehre erwies. Eingang mit dem Familienwappen und dem Spruch „Von Generation zu Generation: Misericordia (Gnade / Mitgefühl) denjenigen, die Ihn fürchten".

Dans le cabinet de travail de Lapo, une lettre encadrée (1780) de Léopold, grand-duc de Toscane, rendant hommage à la famille. L'entrée avec le blason et sa devise : « Miséricorde de génération en génération à celui qui Le craint ».

En el estudio de Lapo cuelga enmarcada una carta escrita para honra de la familia por Leopoldo, Gran Duque de la Toscana, en 1780. Recibiáor con escudo de armas y la frase "Misericordia de generación en generación para quien a Él le tema".

Bits and other tack are displayed above a massive fireplace hearkening back to the time when Fonterutoli was a place to change horses.
Next pages: Oak barrels in the modern cellar designed by Lapo's daughter Agnese.

Morsi e finimenti *sulla cappa del camino ricordano il tempo in cui Fonterutoli era una stazione per il cambio dei cavalli.*
Pagina successiva: botti di rovere nella cantina dalle linee moderne, progettata da Agnese, figlia di Lapo.

Das Pferdegeschirr *über dem gewaltigen Kamin erinnert an die Zeit, als man in Fonterutoli die Pferde wechselte.*
Nächste Seite: Eichenfässer im von Lapo Mazzeis Tochter Agnese entworfenen modernen Weinkeller.

Mords et autres pièces *de sellerie, disposés au-dessus de l'énorme cheminée, rappellent l'époque où l'on changeait ici de chevaux.*
Page suivante : quelques barriques en chêne dans la cave moderne conçue par la fille de Lapo, Agnese.

Las bridas y arreos *de caballo expuestos sobre una maciza chimenea aluden a los tiempos en los que este lugar era una parada de postas.*
Página siguiente: barricas de roble en la moderna bodega diseñada por Agnese, la hija de Lapo.

Imprint

All photographs by Etienne Hunyady

Texts Kelley F. Hurst
Introduction Marco Fini
Translations & Copy-editing Durante & Zoratti, Cologne
Jacquelyn Poarch
(English/Introduction)
Matteo Mazzacurati,
Chiara Pagnani (Italian)
Mechthild Barth,
Alessandra Cacace (German)
Virginie de Bermond-Gettle,
Virginie Paumier (French)
Almudena Sassiain Calle,
Santiago Navarro (Spanish)

Editorial Coordination Arndt Jasper, teNeues Verlag
Production Nele Jansen, teNeues Verlag
Design Christina Naumann,
vierzehn02, Munich
Color Separation Laudert GmbH & Co. KG, Vreden

Published by teNeues Publishing Group

teNeues Verlag GmbH + Co. KG
Am Selder 37, 47906 Kempen, Germany
Tel.: 0049-(0)2152-916-0, Fax: 0049-(0)2152-916-111
Press department: arehn@teneues.de

teNeues International Sales Division
Speditionstraße 17, 40221 Düsseldorf, Germany
Tel.: 0049-(0)211-994597-0, Fax: 0049-(0)211-994597-40

teNeues Publishing Company
16 West 22nd Street, New York, N.Y. 10010, USA
Tel.: 001-212-627-9090, Fax: 001-212-627-9511

teNeues Publishing UK Ltd.
P.O. Box 402, West Byfleet KT14 7ZF, Great Britain
Tel.: 0044-1932-4035-09, Fax: 0044-1932-4035-14

teNeues *France* S.A.R.L.
93, rue Bannier, 45000 Orléans, France
Tel.: 0033-2-3854-1071, Fax: 0033-2-3862-5340

www.teneues.com

Bibliographic information published by Die Deutsche
Bibliothek. Die Deutsche Bibliothek lists this publication
in the Deutsche Nationalbibliografie; detailed bibliographic
data is available in the Internet at http://dnb.ddb.de.

Acknowledgements

"I would like to thank all the families who participated in this book. Most of all I thank Marisa who believed in this project; Sibilla who gave me "vital information"; Lithe who gave me great ideas; and Manni, without whom I wouldn't have done this book."

Etienne Hunyady